An American Unsung

Based on Actual Events In the Life of My Friend, Dayton Edie, American Hero

Harold Ray Finley, Jr.

Edited by Carol Greer

Hoosick Falls, New York
2019

First published in 2019 by the Merriam Press

Third Edition (2020)

Copyright © 2019 by Harold Ray Finley, Jr.
Book design by Ray Merriam
Additional material copyright of named contributors.

All rights reserved.
No part of this book may be used or reproduced in any manner whatsoever without written permission, except in the case of brief quotations embodied in critical articles or reviews.

The unauthorized reproduction or distribution of this copyrighted work is illegal. Criminal copyright infringement, including infringement without monetary gain, is investigated by the FBI and is punishable by up to five years in federal prison and a fine of $250,000.

The views expressed are solely those of the author.

ISBN 978-0-359-57097-3
Library of Congress Control Number 2019931639

This work was designed, produced, and published in
the United States of America by the

Merriam Press
489 South Street
Hoosick Falls NY 12090

E-mail: ray@merriam-press.com
Web site: merriam-press.com

Dedication

This book is dedicated to Joseph Michael Littlefield, my first grandchild. He is my parent's first great grandchild and my four grandparent's first great-great grandchild. Joseph, I hope you grow up in a world that never needs brave men like Dayton Edie, but I hope you will be such a man should your country ever call.

Contents

Foreword 7
Soldier 9

Beginnings of a Combat Soldier 10
Befriending a Ballplayer 17
Dogs and the Lesson Learned 19
School Days are Over 23
Hog Killing and Beer 25
Trying to Enlist 27
Baseball 29
He's Not in the Navy Now 31
Early Training 35
Specialized Training 37
The Yanks are Coming Again! 41
Digging for Details 47
Leading up to a Forgotten Battle 51
Above and Beyond 57
The Professor and Stacker 61
A Medal of Honor Thrown Away 63
Capture and Escape 71
Fighting in a Churchill 75
Close Calls and Bridges 79
Twice Wounded 83
Generals Disobeying Orders 85
Nazis 89
The General's Favorite Stable Boy 97

Boots and Amputation Orders 103
Marta 107
CARE 113
Liberated by the Enemy 115
Skills of a Farmer Turned Soldier 119
Road Trips to Yugoslavia 123
One Edie Becomes Three 129
Watching an A-bomb Explode 139
Psychic Sergeant 143
Back to the States 153
Marching with Martin Luther King, Jr. 157
Last Meeting with Dizzy Dean 161
One Retirement Down, One to Go 163
Tragedy 179
The Knee Accident 183
Meeting the Edies 185
Fox Holes and Cat Holes 189
The Last Dates 191
Excuses and Explanations 195

Appendices

Medals and Honors 199
Battalions, Divisions, and HQs Dayton Served 201
Special Orders and Security Clearances 205

Foreword

Dayton Edie (say it with a long E, like the ice cream) was my good friend and a bona fide American hero. He seldom spoke of his own combat from fighting in World War II and the Korean War, and on those rare occasions that he did, I listened intently. Although his own actions rarely came up, now and then he would discuss historic events and famous people encountered during his lifetime, and this story is as Dayton told it.

Some of Dayton's experiences occurred when he was an operative for the Office of Strategic Services (OSS) and the Counter Intelligence Corps (CIC), covert branches of the U.S. government. Of these, he almost never spoke. The stories you find here about those covert activities are based on vague narratives and hedged comments from Dayton, combined with the results of years of in-depth research. There is not a doubt in my mind he was a member of both organizations during his long career in the U.S. military.

This biography has been a labor of love. Dayton was a true American hero, but he is a hero unsung. Read, and decide for yourself if he doesn't deserve to be remembered for his courage under fire, his leadership, his strength, and ultimately his kindness, since history has all but forgotten Dayton Edie.

Soldier

I was that which others did not want to be.

I went where others feared to go, and did what others failed to do.

I asked nothing from those who gave nothing, and reluctantly accepted the thought of eternal loneliness---should I fail.

I have seen the face of terror; felt the stinging cold of fear; and enjoyed the sweet taste of a moment's love.

I have cried, pained, and hoped---but most of all,

I have lived times others would say were best forgotten.

At least someday I will be able to say that I was proud of what I was---

a soldier.

—George L. Skypeck

used with permission of author

All rights reserved

Beginnings of a Combat Soldier

In late December 1944, American soldiers rushed to the aid of a 19 year old private named Dayton Edie. Dayton's fellow soldiers were trying to get him out of sight and far away from General George S. "Blood and Guts" Patton. It was their hope they could keep the young hero from being court-martialed. Their efforts saved a unique military career, which by the time he retired from the U.S. Army had spanned 23 years.

Before his confrontation with Patton, Pfc. Dayton Edie had been nominated for the Medal of Honor for his heroic actions at the Battle of the Bulge. The recommendation for the medal was never sent to the United States Congress for final approval, because it was shredded by General Patton himself. Let me tell you something of my friend, Dayton Edie, prior to his run-in with the great general.

Dayton Edie was born in Cincinnati, Ohio on the 9th of February 1925. Dayton was given no middle name or initial. He was the son of Clarence and Lucille Edie. Lucille bore Dayton with the help of a midwife at a boarding house in Cincinnati. His father, Clarence, was born in Kansas City, Kansas, while his mother was a native of Morehead, Kentucky. Dayton was of Scotch Irish descent, and he inherited some French from a great grandmother. His great grandfather met his French great grandmother on a ship that brought them both to America. The two grandparents met and married on that same ship in 1850.

Clarence Edie had been a coal miner since his youth and had worked in the mines almost 30 years. Clarence was athletic enough to try out for the 1912 U.S. Olympics Swim Team.

A future general named Patton competed in the Pentathlon during the same 1912 Olympics in Stockholm, Sweden.

Unfortunately, a mining accident resulted in a horrible fracture to Clarence's right leg just below the knee. Due to the injury, Dayton's father was unable to compete in the Olympics, and ever afterwards Clarence Wate Edie experienced great difficulty walking. The accident not only ended his Olympic dreams, it also drove Clarence out of the coal mines forever. To earn money near

Pittsburgh and along the Ohio River, Clarence built a houseboat and became a commercial fisherman. From then on Dayton's father primarily fished for white perch, jack salmon, catfish, paddle fish (which had no bones), carp and eel to support his family.

Clarence Edie and his family stayed on the river and lived in the houseboat, eventually leaving Pittsburgh and traveling to Lawrenceburg, Indiana. From there they traveled down the Ohio River near the Kentucky cities of Foster and Maysville. During this time, the family made money fishing and trapping on the banks of the Ohio River.

Between the ages of five and six, when Dayton was old enough to attend school, his father bought a farm in Carntown, Kentucky. Clarence purchased the 100 acre farm primarily so his son could attend school in Carntown's one-room schoolhouse. Dayton said it was the same one-room schoolhouse Jackie Robinson had attended in his youth.

Clarence Edie married ten times over the course of his life. Every few years his wife would pack up and leave. Not long after, the previous wife would be replaced by a new one. Even though most of these ex-wives re-married, Clarence managed to remain friends with the ladies who had carried his name.

Lucille Edie, by leaving Clarence had also left Dayton causing a strong bond to forge between father and son. He never fully explained but even if Dayton was out of touch with his mother, at the very least he must have kept tabs on her because he knew the year in which Lucille died.

Carntown was between 40 and 50 miles from Cincinnati, but it was located on the Kentucky side of the Ohio River in Pendleton County. The Edies left the houseboat and moved into a farmhouse on the property Clarence purchased. A later military form has the property with an address of Route 1 Box 89, Pendleton, Kentucky.

A number of step-mothers rotated in and out at the farmhouse. Dayton also lived with a half-sister named Ethel for a short time and later with a cousin named Albert. Albert Edie moved in with Dayton and Clarence after Albert's father, Clarence's brother, passed away. Dayton's cousin Albert lived in the farmhouse until he was drafted into the U.S. Army in early 1941. Dayton and Albert grew up through the Great Depression and experienced the hard side of life as they leaned on one another.

By the time he was seven in 1932, Dayton was regularly hunting with a .22 rifle. He got his first shotgun, a 20 gauge, at nine years old. Eventually, he also acquired a 12 gauge and a 16 gauge shotgun. He kept only the 20 gauge throughout his lifetime. Sometime while he was stationed overseas, all his other weapons were stolen from his father's house.

Dayton trapped many animals primarily for their pelts, mainly muskrat, mink, raccoon, possum, fox, and weasel. Other animals were hunted for food, such as rabbit, squirrel, quail, and dove. Dayton said even groundhog was edible if fixed properly. (Don't tell Punxsutawney Phil!) At that time, most deer had been run off or killed. The rabbit and squirrel populations were slim. He said he often had to hunt all day to bag between six and eight small animals, barely enough to keep food on the table.

Dayton also hunted duck, geese, and wild turkey when they were in season. All the hunting and trapping at such an early age turned him into a skilled hunter and an expert shot. He was well-versed with every available weapon, and he made good use of the skills he acquired during the Great Depression on behalf of the United States government many years later.

In 1933 at the heart of the Depression, Dayton was eight and used money he earned from animal skins and pelts to pay for his own clothes.

"At least what clothes I had anyway," said Dayton.

Today it is considered quite a feat for an eight year old boy to take care of himself, but Dayton said back then it was just the way things were. "An eight year old had to grow up fast if he wanted to survive." He said parents usually bought their children bib overalls that were expected to last a number of years.

Anything else they wanted, they had to earn money to buy.

The male head of household also got the lion's share of the food during the Depression years. With most of the male population doing physical jobs and food in short supply, the men ate the meat because they needed the protein to complete the tasks required of them. Children usually received only old biscuits and gravy. At the beginning of every meal, Dayton said he made sure to save a piece of bread for later. This bread was used to wipe the plate when they finished eating. With food scarce, he said "You always completely cleaned your plate, because leaving anything was considered as bad as sin!"

Out one day to check his traps, Dayton got a little more than he expected after coming across a tripped snarl line. The line went down into a hole, and when Dayton pulled on it there was movement which indicated the animal was still alive. It took him only a few seconds to pull the line up out of the hole and realize he was facing the business end of a very angry skunk, which promptly did what skunks do and blasted him!

Dayton received quite a spray. The skunk paid dearly but that didn't help remove the stench that stubbornly stuck to Dayton for weeks, particularly around his face. This happened when Dayton was in the fourth or fifth grade and attending the one-room schoolhouse in Carntown. The other children wanted Dayton banned from school until the horrible stench dissipated. Instead of being sent home however, the teacher made him sit in the back of class. It took more than two weeks for Dayton to rejoin his friends in his regular seat.

Dayton's Father, Clarence Edie.

Clarence Edie at home in Kentucky.

Befriending a Ballplayer

Dayton saw the legendary Dizzy Dean play baseball for the first time when he was 5 years old. At eight in 1933, Dayton met the future Hall of Fame player at a Cincinnati Reds game. The Reds were hosting the St. Louis Cardinals, Dean's team at the time. Dayton and his cousin, Albert, were walking around the ballpark at Redland Field when they simply bumped into Dizzy Dean.

Redland Field was renamed Crosley Field a year later in 1934. In those days the ballplayers intermingled with the fans before game time, something modern baseball fans can't begin to imagine.

When the two boys happened upon Dizzy Dean, the ballplayer noticed Dayton's curly blonde hair. Dizzy Dean liked Dayton's blonde curls and rubbed his hands through Dayton's hair. The St. Louis pitcher told the two boys, "I sure would like a beer."

Albert ignored the hint. He was a Cincinnati Reds fan, and he was only there to see his beloved team. Dayton was a Reds fan too, but he was also a fan of Dizzy Dean. The Cardinal pitcher had made a strong impression on the little boy three years earlier. Dayton decided it wouldn't hurt the Reds too much if he got just one beer for the Cardinal star. He left and returned a short time later with a beer for the baseball great. That single beer started a lifelong friendship and a tradition both observed until Dayton joined the Army in 1943. Every time Dayton attended a game when Dizzy Dean was playing, he got two beers for the ballplayer before game time.

Prohibition had just ended. At that time laws about the sale of alcohol varied widely from state to state and in many cases were not enforced at all. Dayton later said the only thing that kept children from purchasing alcohol was the occasional bartender with a guilty conscience. Even that didn't happen often since it was the Depression, and bartenders wanted money any way they could get it. It was also a common practice in some areas for parents to send a child to the bar to pick beer up for them. Dayton had no difficulty buying the cold beers for his idol.

Dayton and Cardinal Manager, Frankie Frisch, could never figure out what Dizzy Dean did with those beers. Cardinal uniforms had no pockets and were not loose enough to conceal a bottle. Dayton tried many times to see what Dean did with the beer after Dayton handed it over, but he never did figure it out. Frisch also said he never caught Dizzy Dean with the beer at a game, or there might have been trouble for the future Hall of Famer. Frisch frowned on drinking before games. It's possible the thirsty pitcher downed the beers quickly with no one looking, but Dayton said he watched for that and never saw it.

For years Dayton honored their unspoken agreement and always had two beers waiting for Dizzy Dean at Crosley Field.

Dizzy Dean played for the St. Louis Cardinals in 1930 and from 1932- 1937. He is enshrined in the Major League Baseball Hall of Fame having held several Cardinal and major league records, some of which still stand today.

Dogs and the Lesson Learned

As a youngster, and until he joined the Army, Dayton had a huge dog. It was black and white like a beagle, but the dog's father was a huge coon dog.

Because he was so big, they named him Ferdinand after the giant bull. Ferdinand was at Dayton's side on many adventures.

One particular morning however, Dayton went out alone without Ferdinand. After messing around in the woods and coming out in the open, he found himself along a tall wooden fence. The tall fence was made of boards woven together to form a barrier.

As he walked the fence, a pack of wild dogs appeared out of nowhere.

Suddenly there were about six vicious dogs all barking and snapping at him. The only thing Dayton had carried for protection on this adventure was a tobacco stick. He began fighting hard, swinging the stick to fend off the vicious dogs. It was rare for him not to have a real weapon handy, and Ferdinand was as big as three of the wild dogs put together, but Dayton had left both at home. He swung that tobacco stick like a madman to keep the dogs at bay. All the while, he continued to back up to the fence. He reached the fence, grabbed the top, and pulled himself up and over.

Thankfully, the dogs could not climb the fence, and once he landed on the other side, Dayton said, "I ran home faster than any time before or since." After that encounter Dayton never went in the woods again without either the faithful Ferdinand or a weapon by his side. Usually both!

During the Great Flood of 1937, Dayton learned an important lesson—one he felt helped him during his military career and later in life. The '37 Flood had lifted up whole houses and sent them floating downstream, eventually making it all the way to the river. Sitting on the banks of the Ohio River, Dayton and his cousin Albert had watched as house after house floated past. Some of the houses were floating bottom side up, while others floated on their sides. A few of the houses floated upright with their foundations right at the water line and looked completely normal other than the fact the house was floating down the river.

Most of the houses floating downstream had sunk down to their attics leaving only the tips of their roofs exposed.

Many of the owners of these houses had put their valuables in the attics hoping to protect their possessions from the flood. Of course the owners had never dreamed the flood waters would rise high enough to lift an entire house and carry it away!

Dayton, who was 12 at the time, and Albert sat watching as those houses floated by. They knew there were probably valuables in most of them. In search of treasure, the two boys decided to brave the dangers of the flood and swim out to the floating houses to explore.

The boys jumped into the river and swam to the first house, which had only the attic above water. Dayton was the smaller of the two, so he climbed into the attic window while Albert sat on the roof. Even in the attic, water was up to Dayton's waist. Dayton realized the situation was much more dangerous than either had imagined. He wanted to quickly grab anything of value and get out!

There were all kinds of things floating around, including furniture.

Dayton grabbed the first thing that caught his eye, a small box. The small box was on top of a table that was floating around inside the attic. He picked something else up, and then spotting another item he wanted, he dropped the first thing he'd grabbed and lost it in the dark waters of the attic. With all the different things floating past, he couldn't make up his mind, so this went on - dropping one thing to grab another as the house floated along, creaking and groaning. A sudden jolt got Dayton's attention. He was certain the house was going to sink and take him with it.

Dayton decided to get out with whatever he was carrying at the time. He climbed out of the attic and onto the roof wishing he still had the first thing he'd started with; a small wooden jewelry box. Dayton told Albert he was done treasure hunting. If Albert wanted anything, he would have to go into the attic to get it himself. Albert thought better of it and decided the risk wasn't worth the reward. The boys jumped off the roof into the river and slowly swam back to shore.

Back on land, and worn out from risking his life for a few trinkets worth nothing, Dayton found himself wishing he'd held on to the small jewelry box. Dayton learned a lesson that day he remembered the rest of his life.

"Always go with your first instinct, because most of the time that first feeling from your gut tends to be right."

It was a life's lesson he drew on many times in the years to come, including decisive decisions made at the Battle of the Bulge.

A young Dayton.

School Days Are Over

Dayton continued his education at Carntown's one-room schoolhouse until the one-room schools were replaced by a single large school, in this case Mount Harbon. Dayton attended Mount Harbon for seventh and eighth grade. After two years there, his father had a stroke which forced Dayton to leave school to provide for the family. While Clarence Edie convalesced, his young son focused on the survival of the family and the farm. Dayton eventually earned his General Equivalency Diploma (G.E.D.) during his service in the U.S. Army.

In 1938 at 13, Dayton worked full-time and then some. Dayton took any odd job he could find, no matter how tough, terrible, or physically challenging it was.

On one of his Army reenlistment forms it indicates Dayton had worked a 100 acre farm from 1938-1943. Dayton had been an all-around farmhand, and he knew just about every aspect of farming. He planted and dug potatoes. He cultivated and harvested corn, tobacco, beans, okra, eggplant, onions, squash, peppers, and tomatoes. Along with raising crops, he also cared for livestock, cut wood, mended fence, repaired farm buildings, and worked a two horse team. He even harvested sorghum for making molasses. Not bad for a teenager.

Dayton continued to trap and hunt animals for food and the pelts they provided. He was one of the best shots around. Old widows gave him shotgun shells, since they knew their ammo wouldn't be wasted if it was in Dayton's capable hands. He'd hunt with their ammo and bring back either a rabbit or a squirrel for the widow's evening meal. In exchange for doing the hunting, the women would give him a portion of the cooked meat.

Dayton was certainly an expert marksman after relying on his hunting skills for so many years to survive. Each shot had to be on target to maximize the scarce ammo. This was a skill that added immeasurably to his success in the military.

Having grown up around the Cincinnati, Ohio area, Dayton understood and spoke a great deal of German and Italian. Cincinnati is known for its large population of German immigrants as well as Italians. Being multilingual, a marksman, and blessed with a high IQ probably all influenced his eventual entry into the Office of Strategic Services (OSS) and from there the very secretive Counter Intelligence Corps (CIC).

Old folks used to say if a baby bird comes out of its nest early it's not likely to make it. If it does manage to survive, it will probably end up being one of the strongest and smartest in the flock. Dayton Edie became one smart, tough old bird.

Clarence and Dayton on the river.

Hog Killing and Beer

One of the brutal jobs Dayton took on during the Depression was slaughtering hogs for his neighbors. Killing a hog is neither pleasant nor easy. Dayton did the job because it paid a few pennies he wouldn't have had otherwise. At a time when he was struggling to support his family, he said, "Any amount of money, little or not, was important."

Every part of a hog is either eaten or used in some way.

After learning the hard way on the first few, Dayton eventually became the best in town at taking down hogs. Killing a hog is actually a very difficult task. Bullets were seldom used because they were too valuable and were needed for hunting wild animals. Instead of shooting them, Dayton used a board with a long thick three to four inch nail sticking out of one end. After jumping on the animal's back, Dayton would drive the nail up and into the pig to pierce its brain and bring it down.

Today, people might be upset at the slaughter of a hog but during the Depression people were always hungry. They could not be sentimental about a creature capable of feeding their family for months.

Many of the tools Dayton used as a boy were made by his Uncle Rath.

Rath was a blacksmith which was a highly respected vocation in those days. John Rath could repair or build just about anything. Dayton learned a lot at his knee.

The suggestion for the board and spike came from Uncle Rath.

At one point Uncle Rath decided it was time to replace his old boat with a new one. He planned on buying a new boat until he found out how much they cost. Uncle Rath was tight with his money, and he did not spend it unless he absolutely had to. The boats for sale all cost $85 and up. Seeing the price, Rath said "After paying $20 for my first boat, I'm not about to pay $85 now!"

It had been over 30 years since his uncle had paid $20 for the boat he was replacing. His uncle refused to allow for inflation and told the boat salesman he would just build it himself, and that is exactly what he did. Uncle Rath built a boat in the basement of his house. After taking a year to finish it, he asked a bunch of men to come help him bring the boat out of the basement. Unfortunately, Rath had forgotten to double check his measurements, and no matter how they tried, that boat would not fit through the doors. Dayton said, "That boat ended up being the prettiest potato bin ever made."

Dayton Edie had his first beer at age 10. Years later he said that besides Albert, one of his favorite drinking buddies was a guy named Clooney. In the northern hills of Kentucky, old Andy Clooney apparently came every weekend from a couple counties over and spent Saturday and Sunday night drinking with his friends in Carntown, especially his buddy Dayton Edie. Dayton's drinking pal was none other than the father of the beautiful and talented Rosemary Clooney and grandfather to well-known actor George Clooney.

Trying to Enlist

A few months prior to the surprise attack at Pearl Harbor on the 7th December 1941, Dayton Edie tried to enlist in the armed services. He was 16 years old. His cousin Albert had already been drafted, and Dayton wanted to join up as well. He walked to the local courthouse in Carntown and found an old clerk to wait on him. The clerk at the courthouse was Ira E. Yelton, who had worked as a clerk for some time, at least as long as Dayton could remember.

"How can I help you?" asked Ira.

Dayton told him he was there to enlist.

"You have to be at least 21 years old to enlist," answered Ira.

"Well, then I'm 21, and I'm here to enlist," he exclaimed.

Looking directly at him, Ira said, "Dayton, I just sold you a hunting license, and I know how old you are. Now go back home!"

A dejected Dayton did as Ira said and went home still a civilian.

Albert Edie was drafted into the U.S. Army before the United States entered World War II. Due to rising tensions in the world, the draft had been instated about a year before the attack on Pearl Harbor. There is no available record of where or for how long Albert Edie served, but he did survive the war. Albert died of cancer in the middle of the 1990s.

Dayton learned of the Japanese attack on Pearl Harbor from Uncle Rath. Dayton came out of the woods after a day of hunting with old Ferdinand near his uncle's house and noticed him on his porch. Uncle Rath yelled to Dayton that "The Japs bombed Pearl Harbor!" Uncle Rath had heard the news like many Americans from radio announcements describing the attack.

Days after Pearl Harbor, a huge wave of new recruits all volunteered for the armed forces of the United States of America. These early recruits suffered horrible losses with only 40% of them returning from the war uninjured.

One consequence of the heavy casualties in the early months of the war was that the minimum age requirement for enlistment dropped. First the minimum age went to 20, then 19, and eventually dropped to 18.

Dayton was only 17 and a half, so he was still under the requirement for enlistment, but old Ira Yelton had retired, and with the age requirement closer to his actual age, Dayton decided to try again. A new, much younger clerk had taken Ira's place. Dayton went to the courthouse in Carntown a second time and told the new clerk he was there to enlist. The new clerk looked Dayton up and down and then got up from his desk and left the room, leaving Dayton standing there to wonder what was going on. A short time later, the young clerk returned and said, "The old man says you're still not old enough and to go on home."

Old Ira Yelton may have retired, but he was still there and still in charge! Dayton left the courthouse frustrated, having failed a second time to enlist in the armed services.

Baseball

Like many boys who grew up during the Depression, Dayton played baseball any time he could. He mainly played left field, but as a utility player he played where needed. He was good enough to join a team called the California Crossroads. This team was located in California, Kentucky and was sponsored by a local tavern. Later he played for another team named The Green Lines, sponsored by a bus company in Newport, Kentucky. By 1941, Dayton was a non-roster player for the Huntington, West Virginia baseball team. Huntington would have been what Single A ball is today. Back then it was known as either C or D ball. Non-roster players were called scrubs. A scrub got to play only if needed, and he was only paid for the days he played. Once Dayton got there and was able to join the team, he said "I was able to play almost every day."

Dayton's old friend Dizzy Dean came by and watched him play while he was with the Huntington Club. At that time, Dean was scouting for the St. Louis Cardinals and saw enough talent in Dayton to recommend another scout from the Cardinals come to evaluate him. The scout who came was Billy Southworth.

Dayton never knew that Billy was the manager of the St. Louis Cardinals, a man who would go on to be a legend in St. Louis. After watching Dayton play, Southworth followed Dayton to a saloon near the ballpark. Southworth told Dayton he wanted him to report to Winston Salem in early 1942. Winston Salem was a farm team for the St. Louis Cardinals. The Cardinals' manager bought Dayton a sandwich and a beer, then left, telling him to be sure and report to Winston Salem that spring. He ate the sandwich and drank the beer, but when the spring of 1942 arrived Dayton never went to Winston Salem. He figured the scout had just been doing a favor for his old pal, Dizzy Dean and was only being nice. Plus Dayton didn't have money for a trip like that.

Shortly after the 1942 spring tryouts, Southworth returned to Huntington. The Cardinals' manager found Dayton in the saloon and was extremely upset with him for not having reported to Winston Salem. Dayton explained to Billy that he hadn't believed him, and more importantly, that he didn't have money for a train ride to Winston Salem, less yet for the hotel stay once he arrived.

To convince Dayton he was sincere, Billy decided to create a contract for them to sign. Southworth took a brown paper sack and wrote on it, "Dayton Edie to report to Cardinal Farm team in Florida." Then he signed his name and gave Dayton $60. Billy handed Dayton the paper sack and the money, and this time he paid for two ham sandwiches and a beer. Before leaving, Southworth told Dayton not to forget to report to the farm team in Florida that coming March (1943). Dayton tried to talk him into another beer as part of the deal, but Southworth ignored his plea and left to go scout another prospect.

Dayton did not make it to the Cardinal farm team in Florida. He tried finding Southworth after the war to give the $60 back, but he wasn't quite sure of the name never having realized the actual manager of the St. Louis Cardinals had scouted him. Dayton must have been a talented player for his friend Dizzy Dean to endorse him and for Billy Southworth to order him twice to the upper Cardinal farm teams. And remember, $60 was a lot of money in the 1940's.

The contract on the brown paper bag was lost after Dayton enlisted.

Instead of traveling to Florida and trying out for the St. Louis Cardinals, Dayton joined the U.S. Army to fight against tyranny and oppression during World War II.

He's Not In the Navy Now

In late January 1943, Dayton was still determined to join the military. Just before his 18th birthday, he bypassed the local courthouse and went to the main recruiting station in Cincinnati, Ohio. In order to qualify for the military, a man had to be at least 18 years old, five feet tall, and weigh a minimum of 105 pounds.

The recruiter took Dayton's measurements, and never questioned his age which was a huge relief. If his age had still been an issue, Clarence Edie had already agreed to sign a waiver. The other two requirements of height and weight were now the problems.

At that time Dayton stood four eleven and a half and weighed a mere 104.5 pounds, narrowly missing on all three requirements. After checking everything twice, the recruiter looked at him and said, "Son, you don't meet the measurements."

Dayton said, "That recruiter must have seen a tear in my eye and felt sorry for me."

"You really want to join up, don't yah?" the recruiter asked.

"I wouldn't have bothered coming all the way here if I didn't mean to join up," responded Dayton.

The recruiter proceeded to tell Dayton that once a week he made a scale adjustment. He told Dayton that if he could jump three feet in the air, he would make the scale adjustment that day!

Dayton responded by telling the recruiter, "I'll jump as high as I can." The recruiter said jumping two feet would probably get it done, but that Dayton should try for three. Then the recruiter had him jump up onto the scale. At the very top of Dayton's jump the recruiter noted his height. When he landed and the needle sprang forward, the recruiter quickly wrote down his weight. From the leap and bounce, Dayton Edie had grown to five foot two and a solid 115 pounds.

After his sudden increase in size, thanks to the helpful recruiter, Dayton and several other new recruits were told to wait. A naval officer soon arrived, who proceeded to swear all of them into the United States Navy. Following the swearing in, the officer stood by the exit door. He then had the new Navy recruits leave the room single file. Dayton got close to the door when the officer stopped the rest from leaving the room. The officer said that the Navy had its quota, and then left with the men he needed.

Not long after the Navy officer left, a Marine sergeant showed up. The Marine sergeant picked from the remaining men. The sergeant took all but three of the fresh recruits. Dayton was one of those three recruits.

Dayton and the other two men continued to wait. At one point, someone came by and asked if they'd like to join the U.S. Coast Guard. All three declined. Finally an Army major showed up asking the three of them if they were hungry. They'd been waiting quite some time, and they all said they were hungry. The major took the three men with him, first taking them to eat. Afterwards he told them to follow him to a truck and get in. With the major and his driver in the front of the truck and the three fresh recruits in the back, they took off down the road.

After a few hours of riding, Dayton wondered where they were headed. He knew the truck was traveling south, which didn't seem right. The other two recruits believed they were headed to a shipyard in Cincinnati, since all of them had been sworn into the Navy only hours before.

The first time the truck stopped the other two men questioned the Army officer about their destination. Dayton stayed quiet, and let the other two do the talking. His fellow recruits informed the Major that the three of them had been sworn into the United States Navy!

The major barked, "You're all in the United States Army now." He added, "If anyone needs to be sworn in, that's fine, but either way it's going to be the Army!"

None of the three requested a new swearing in. They quickly got back in the truck and traveled south.

Technically during World War II Dayton was never sworn into the U.S. Army and was never released from the U.S. Navy. However, Pvt. Dayton Edie was sworn into the U.S. Army officially at his reenlistment in the summer of 1945.

The way he talked about it years later, half-joking, he believed the Navy still owed him back pay!

Eventually, or inevitably, this same under-aged, under-sized, and under-weight, son of a fisherman ended up at the Battle of the Bulge. There Pvt. Dayton Edie went well above and beyond the call of duty. But first, he had to be trained and turned into an American soldier.

Early Training

A few weeks before his 18th birthday, Dayton had joined the U.S. Army. According to a certified and corrected copy of one military record, Dayton spent time at Ft. Thomas, Kentucky, which is just south of Cincinnati. From Ft. Thomas the recruits went by train to Camp Hood, Texas. Upon their arrival at Camp Hood the recruits were informed there was no place at the camp for them to sleep. All of them were told to get in transport trucks and travel to Camp Bowie.

Unfortunately, when they arrived at Camp Bowie they were told there were no barracks there either. The men had to pitch tents until they could build their own barracks. The only real weapons to train with at Camp Bowie were Thompson sub machine guns and a few .30 caliber Browning machine guns. There were not enough rifles, so instead they used two by fours while learning parade march. The lack of equipment severely limited the training available at Camp Bowie.

The first tank destroyers finally arrived at Camp Hood, and the men at Camp Bowie needed to transfer there in order to receive training. However, at the time there was no transportation available. The officer in charge decided not to wait for trucks, instead ordering his men to march the distance to Camp Hood.

The actual distance between the two camps is approximately 100 miles, but the battalions had to zigzag to avoid population centers. The actual distance traveled ended up being about 150 miles. Five to six battalions made the march to Camp Hood. There were 700 to 800 men in each battalion. Two of the battalions were made up of segregated black soldiers. Each of the battalions had three to four companies with over 200 men per company.

At first the men marched during the day, but the soldiers began dropping from heat stroke. Temperatures during the day rose to 120 degrees. Every soldier was given one canteen of water per day, and they had to make it last. Still, more and more soldiers succumbed to the heat, so they began marching at night from 11 PM until four in the morning. It took about six days for the battalions to march to Camp Hood during the summer of 1943.

At Camp Hood, Dayton trained for the next year and became an expert marksman on every weapon available. He was already an expert marksman from his hunting days, so he quickly learned the specifics of all the new weapons he was given. Dayton said it was the training he received at Camp Hood that proved invaluable to him during the war. He credited that training with saving his life on more than one occasion.

Camp Hood was where Dayton was first schooled in the use of armored vehicles. He trained on an M3 Halftrack which had an exposed French 75mm gun mounted just behind and above the cab. The first fully tracked vehicle he trained on was the M10 Wolverine tank destroyer. During his time in Texas he also trained on the fully-tracked M18 Hellcat and M36 Jackson tank destroyers. Private Dayton Edie trained at Camp Hood until the summer of 1944, having spent approximately a year there being turned into a member of the elite Tank Destroyers!

Tank Destroyer patch.

Specialized Training

Along with weapons training, Dayton received survival training at Camp Hood. Some of the training took place in the desert as the recruits were taught to find water beneath the sand. If you dig deep enough, and know where and how to look for it, there is usually water. Dayton said finding water in the desert generally involved finding a low spot in the sand.

After survival training at Camp Hood, he left Texas traveling to Alabama and Tennessee. There he participated in armored maneuvers where tanks were used to cross a variety of terrains.

Dayton also received more survival training while in the swamps of Alabama. In the swamps he was taught to live off things that you never thought could possibly pass for food. He always said he was amazed at what a man could eat if he had to. Dayton said, "And this came from someone who had been willing to eat just about anything out of necessity during the Depression!"

Before being shipped overseas, Dayton's final training took place at Ft. Jackson, South Carolina. While stationed at Ft. Jackson he learned the skills of a wireman - everything involved in signal and communications. This included being trained on wire, sound, switchboard, and visual signals. He qualified as a Signal Operations Instructions (SOI) operator. A SOI operator could decode incoming messages and code outgoing ones, which required a high level of clearance. Because of this particular qualification, during the war Dayton ended up having direct knowledge of orders sent and received by some very well-known Generals, including the Supreme Allied Commander, General Dwight D. Eisenhower himself.

Dayton was never one to brag about his service, but when he was asked about his possible attachment to various covert agencies during and after the war, he would only smile and look slightly pleased. He once said, "Well, at one time I had the highest level of clearance possible." Dayton then turned and walked away. This was his way of stating he had been in the OSS without directly answering the question.

After the war many OSS operatives would later end up working for the CIA. In Dayton's case, however, after volunteering for the OSS he was then selected by Counter Intelligence Corps (CIC). This transfer to the CIC probably occurred when he proved capable of learning everything in signal and communications.

To qualify as a member of the CIC an individual had to be multilingual and have no less than a 120 IQ. Agents or members of the CIC were actually taken from the cream of the crop, and that is why there were so few of them. Members of the CIC primarily were made up of non-commissioned officers, resulting in some extremely intelligent privates, corporals, and sergeants.

> It was clear that a majority of the CIC's personnel were going to be men of a caliber and ability far above their actual grade and rank.[1]

Mark Hatchel, a World War II historian and author who knew Dayton well, wrote in a newsletter that he had been told by communication sergeant Raymond Hummingbird of the 740th Tank Battalion, a close friend of Dayton, "Dayton was one of the spooks assigned to the 740th in Witzenhausen, Germany so that he could listen and monitor radio conversations."[2]

Mark Hatchel said that during the last 740th Tank Battalion Association reunion he and Dayton had both attended, he finally got the old sergeant to admit of volunteering for the OSS. What Dayton never told Mark, me, or apparently anyone else was the part about ending up in the CIC.

> Agents were required to sign an oath that they would conceal their membership of the CIC at all times, and even from their own families, except in the conduct of official business. The degree of secrecy surrounding the CIC was extreme — infinitely greater than that of the FBI, for example.[3]

---

[1] Ian Sayer and Douglas Botting, *America's Secret Army: The Untold Story Of The Counter Intelligence Corps* (Great Britain: Fontana/Collins, 1990), 26.

[2] Mark Hatchel, *740 Tank Battalion Association Newsletter and Historical Quarterly*, Vol. 11: Rhineland-Ardennes-Central Europe (May 2012) 3.

[3] Sayer and Botting, op.cit., 29.

In his newsletter, Mark Hatchel wrote that at some point he told Dayton somebody should write a book about him. Mark says, "He doubted anyone would believe it—even if he was allowed to tell it."[4]

---

[4] Hatchel, op.cit., 4

The Yanks Are Coming Again!

From Ft. Jackson, South Carolina, Private Dayton Edie traveled to Camp Kilmer, New Jersey. He departed from there on the 1st of December 1944 and arrived in New York City the same day. On the 10th of December, the 605th Tank Destroyer Battalion left the states headed for Europe. Originally, Dayton was assigned to the 655th Tank Destroyer Battalion, but when that battalion was disbanded he moved to the 605th Tank Destroyer Battalion. Once he got to know the men of the 605th T.D. Battalion, Dayton eventually discovered that one third of his company came from areas in eastern Kentucky where he himself had grown up. Those men had also enlisted at the recruiting station in Cincinnati where Dayton had joined up.

Dayton and the others crossed the Atlantic on the speedy Queen Mary, but before setting sail, it briefly appeared he might instead be heading to the Pacific. He was even issued a one-piece Pacific jumpsuit with orders pulling him from the battalion.

The orders again changed and Dayton stayed with the 605th Tank Destroyer Battalion.

Having safely crossed the Atlantic Ocean, Dayton and the entire 605th Tank Destroyer Battalion sailed up the Firth of Clyde, Scotland, to Greenock where they disembarked on the 18th December 1944. Greenock is located near Glasgow.

From there the battalion traveled by train to Leek in North Central England. The battalion was taken by truck to Camp Black Shaw Moor which was in Leek Staffordshire, England.

Private Dayton Edie and the 605th Tank Destroyer Battalion, along with men from other battalions were all in the Leek Staffordshire area for a couple of days when he and 30 other soldiers of an advance party were ordered to Weymouth, England. The 30 soldiers selected came from a variety of different battalions which hints at soldiers who had some kind of specialized skill. Dayton seems to have been the only one assigned to this special group from the 605th T.D. Battalion.

Using a Landing Ship, Tank (LST), the advance party of 30 men left the port of Weymouth and crossed the English Channel.

They landed at secured Utah Beach zone. The 30 soldiers in the advance party then made their way to Le Harve, France en route to Vallequerville, which was about three miles from Yvetot (Hotel De Ville).

Dayton and the other 30 men were escorted by military police using jeeps to get them to the front lines quickly. He said it took about five days to get to the front, leaving England around the 20th of December 1944 and arriving at the front lines around Christmas Day or the day after.

When the Battle of the Bulge began and the new giant Royal King Tigers and other German tanks had initially launched their attack, large numbers of American soldiers fled in retreat. Thousands of others were captured or killed.

At first the Germans rolled through the American lines, but eventually the GIs put up stiffer resistance. In some areas like the southern Belgium town of Bastogne, the Americans fighting there were able to slow the German advance.

In the northern Belgian town of Stoumont, Captain Berry commanding C Company of the 740th Tank Battalion, under orders from Colonel Rubel, raced to the front as men from other units retreated. At this time the 740th Tank Battalion was assisting the 119th Infantry Regiment which badly needed help. "They had had one of their battalions over-run and destroyed."[5]

After encountering the enemy and taking on five German Panthers, the lead tanks of C Company managed to knock out three of the tanks. For the first time during the Battle of the Bulge the enemy was stopped and forced back. This did a lot to boost the confidence of other American forces along the front.

At Bastogne the Screaming Eagles of the 101st Airborne were surrounded and cutoff but refused to surrender. Dayton gave them all the credit in the world for their actions. As a Signal Operating Instructions (SOI) operator who monitored the radio lines, Dayton also mentioned that the Screaming Eagles were literally screaming for help! They held their ground refusing to surrender, but the men of the 101st Airborne were running low or out of key supplies, and they needed relief.

---

[5] Lt. Colonel George Kenneth Rubel, *Daredevil Tankers: The Story of the 740th Tank Battalion, U.S. Army* (Werk Gottingen, Germany: Muster-Scmidt, Ltd.), 56.

Like ammunition, gas, food and other essentials, all along the front camouflage was also in short supply. After the heavy snowfall, American uniforms and tanks stood out in the snow like a sore thumb. Local Belgian citizens donated white sheets to the Americans for camouflaging their tanks and uniforms. These sheets saved untold American lives. Decades later in the 1990s, Dayton and his wife Marta traveled to Belgium to find some of the Belgian people who had donated sheets during the Battle of the Bulge. The Edies brought several white sheets and gave them to the residents to repay them for their thoughtfulness. These people were thrilled by the Edies' gesture, and knew their aid to the Americans during World War II had not been forgotten.

The 740th Tank Battalion is one of the most decorated tank battalions in the history of the U.S. Army. To learn more of this incredible battalion and its actions at the Battle of the Bulge read the books *Daredevil Tankers* by Lt. Colonel George Kenneth Rubel and *Into the Breach* by Paul L. Pearson.

At a location in Belgium near Aubin-Neufchateau there is a monument dedicated to the 740th Tank Battalion. The monument was built and paid for by 740th Tank Battalion members and their families, and is maintained by Belgian citizens. Dayton became a member of the 740th Tank Battalion after the war when he was attached to the unit in the fall of 1945. The names of the members of the 740th Tank Battalion who were killed, along with all the members like Dayton who donated for the cost of the monument, are engraved on it. Belgians also volunteer to care for individual American gravesites. Caring for American graves is such a popular honor in the Low Countries—Belgium, The Netherlands, and Luxemburg—that there is a waiting list to volunteer.

740th Tank Battalion patch.

Memorial to the 740th Tank Battalion at Aubin Neufchateau.
Photo by Jeanluc Hanquet.

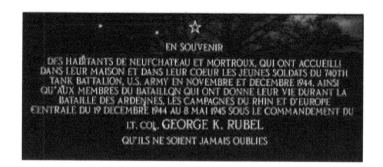

The text on the memorial:

In memory of

The citizens of Neufchâteau and Mortroux, who took into their homes and hearts the young men of the 740th Tank Battalion U.S. Army in November and December, 1944 and to the members of the battalion who gave their lives in the battle of the Ardennes, the Rhineland and Central Europe. Campaigns from December 19, 1944 to May 8, 1945 under command of

LT. Col. George K. Rubel

May they never be forgotten

Digging for Details

Dayton occasionally gave history lessons on many subjects, including general information about the Battle of the Bulge. However, he only discussed his own actions at the Battle of the Bulge three times over a twenty year period.

The first time was around the year 1990. I had known Dayton and his wife, Marta for a few years. I usually went once or twice a month to help out around the yard. I knew Dayton had fought at the Battle of the Bulge, but when I first saw this small, unassuming old man with glasses and a limp, it was tough to imagine him killing a housefly, less yet German soldiers.

On this particular visit, I walked into their house to find Dayton sitting at the dining room table drinking coffee. I sat across from him. With a smile on his face he pushed a copy of Army Times to me. He pointed to a specific article and said, "Read that one."

The article was really just a question written by a veteran from Texas, responding to an article about reunions that Dayton had posted in a previous issue of Army Times. The Texas veteran's question was short and to the point. He asked, "Are you the same Edie who knocked out two Tiger tanks by himself during the Battle of the Bulge?"

I looked up to see Dayton quietly sipping his coffee and wearing a grin from ear to ear.

I was astonished and said, "Mr. Edie, you knocked out two Tiger tanks by yourself?"

He bent down and laced up his boots. Then Dayton stood up. Still grinning, he picked up his cup of coffee and finished it off without saying a word.

"How did you do it?" I asked.

"Probably just got lucky," he answered. That is all he said. I followed him from the kitchen to the garage and then to the backyard, and I felt as if I was walking behind the Audie Murphy nobody knew about.

I was dying to know the details, and asked, "For knocking out the tanks didn't you at least get a medal, like the Medal of Honor?"

"They put me in for the Medal of Honor," Dayton answered.

After a brief pause I couldn't help myself from asking, "And you didn't get it?" "People get angry and jealous and lose paperwork," he answered. The grin disappeared from his face. Something had obviously happened that still angered him.

I let it cool off a bit and then asked Dayton if he would talk to a historian or reporter. To my disappointment but not my surprise Dayton asked me not to contact anyone about his actions during the Battle of the Bulge. I obeyed his wishes and never contacted anyone.

He was comfortable that he had received all the accolades he needed from the recognition of his fellow soldiers.

"What accolades could possibly replace the Medal of Honor?" I asked.

"Nicknames," answered Dayton.

"What kind of nicknames?" I asked

"The other soldiers called me the Professor and the Stacker," he answered proudly. I quickly asked what the nicknames meant.

"Professional Killer and Stacker of Bodies," he answered. He seemed disappointed I hadn't figured out the meanings myself, and he also seemed tired and irritated. I could tell he did not want to talk about it, so I let it go. That was the last question I asked about the Battle of the Bulge for two years.

The second time he talked about the Battle of the Bulge, it was a visit in which the day's work was hard and physical, and the heat index was way up. Our task that day was digging up an old tree stump. The hole from the stump was wide and deep, but in order to bury debris in it later, Dayton wanted the hole even deeper. When the job was done we relaxed on the edge of the hole with our legs dangling down.

Out of nowhere, I asked Dayton again about his actions at the Battle of the Bulge. I just hoped he wouldn't say it was none of my business.

"Mr. Edie, how did you knock out those two Tiger tanks?"

He didn't say much, but he did give a few more details like it had actually been a Tiger tank and a Panther tank, not two Tiger tanks as the veteran had mentioned in the Army Times magazine.

He also said the Tiger tank was the closer of the two and had been facing directly at him. The Panther tank had been farther away and had its side fully exposed. He finished by saying that he knocked the Tiger tank out first and followed up by taking out the Panther. Then in a chopping way he slapped his hands together like that was all there was to it, and he was done talking about it.

Leading Up to a Forgotten Battle

The third and final time Dayton Edie spoke about the Battle of the Bulge was around 2003. Over 10 years had passed since we'd sat in that hole together and he'd last talked about his part in the battle. On three visits during a two week period, he allowed me to question him. I had known Dayton for almost 20 years, and he finally gave me permission to get the real answers on his role in World War II.

On the first of these visits we covered his early years, including how he had entered the service. My questions for him the first night were not difficult, mostly details from his boyhood. A couple of weeks later on the second visit, Dayton talked about things he hadn't spoken of for almost 60 years.

That night, I went there knowing questions were going to be asked about the Battle of the Bulge, and I was not quite sure what to expect. Dayton was never comfortable talking about his own heroic deeds. The tears that rolled down his face by night's end clearly indicated how hard it had been for him to talk about that battle. This story came directly from Dayton himself.

Arriving at the front and by being a good machine gunner, Dayton had been absorbed into the 38th Armored Infantry Battalion. His location was approximately one mile from the town of St. Vith.

The Belgian town of St. Vith is located on the German border, and at the northern opposite end from Bastogne. Even though St. Vith was in Belgium, the inhabitants spoke German because of their proximity to Germany.

The Americans in that area were holding the line and anticipating a German attack, when suddenly the crew of an M18 Hellcat Tank Destroyer managed to stray into no-man's land. Shortly after the Hellcat got lost it was hit by an enemy shell. All of this happened right in front of Dayton's position on the frontline.

The Hellcat had gone into a small patch of woods, and the second the crew stuck its nose out the other side, it was blasted by an enemy shell. Dayton had watched the American tank destroyer go into the woods and heard the explosion of the shell. Believing the Hellcat had been hit in the chassis and that it might explode, the crew jumped out and abandoned their disabled tank destroyer. They raced back to the American lines, expecting to hear an explosion right behind them.

But the shell had struck the Hellcat in its tracks, not actually hitting the hull and chassis. If the crew had known that, they might have at least brought back some of the 40 to 50 high explosive shells inside the Hellcat. Ammo was in short supply, and the shells were extremely valuable. Once the crew made it back to the American line, their sergeant strongly urged them to retrieve the ammo.

Dayton was manning a machine gun, and happened to be right there when the crew returned to the American lines. He heard the angry sergeant trying to convince his men to go back for the shells. Dayton asked them, "Why didn't you guys just bring the shells back with you in the first place, instead of worrying about them now?"

The tanker crew paid no attention to Dayton, nor could the sergeant persuade them to return to their abandoned Hellcat tank destroyer. They refused to retrieve the high explosive shells or do anything else that involved returning to the Hellcat. Instead they told the sergeant they were headed off to find their own unit.

Shortly after the crew and their sergeant left, Dayton requested permission to go to the Hellcat himself to see what could be done. He volunteered to reconnoiter the enemy and possibly retrieve some of the precious shells. He was granted permission, and by mostly staying low and crawling through the heavy snow, he made his way unseen by the enemy to the wooded patch of trees where the abandoned Hellcat sat motionless. The M18 Hellcat turret has no top armor, leaving it open and unprotected. While trying not to be seen, Dayton crawled up the rear of the Hellcat's turret and quickly slid down into it. Inside the Hellcat the precious high explosive shells lay abandoned.

Between the American and German lines were many small wooded areas.

The Hellcat was in one of these wooded areas and did not face the enemy positions directly but sat at somewhat of an angle with its cannon and front hull protruding slightly to the left. Directly in front of the Hellcat was a road horizontal to the tank's position going out to its left and right.

Just down that road some 100 yards to the left of the Hellcat, another road connected to form a crossroads. This connecting road came directly from across the field, emerging from a tree line of dense woods that were around 400 yards away from Dayton and the Hellcat. The thickest foliage was on the right side of the road.

From the middle of no-man's land, Dayton sat in the Hellcat trying to figure out the best way to carry those shells back to American lines. He hadn't been in the tank destroyer long, when a giant Royal King Tiger tank suddenly emerged from the woods and out into the open. When it first appeared the Royal King Tiger tank was about 400 yards away from the Hellcat, and just down from the left side of the road that divided the woods. Its huge cannon turned toward Dayton and the Hellcat, and from that moment on the gun remained aimed at the American tank destroyer. The big German tank then began moving through the snow, until it reached the road. After driving up onto the road, the Royal King Tiger tank turned and moved slowly toward where the two roads crossed. Sitting in the M18 Hellcat right down from where the roads crossed, Dayton tried to remain calm as the big enemy tank came closer.

At a point some 150 yards away from the Hellcat, the enemy tank stopped with its turret and 88 mm cannon aimed directly at the gun of the Hellcat. The Royal King Tiger tank's hull then turned until its frontal armor also directly faced the Hellcat. The opposing tanks were now in a standoff with their frontal armor and cannons pointing precisely at each other.

A few seconds passed which must have seemed like an eternity to Dayton, but the German tank did not fire. The tanks both sat motionless. The crew of the German King Tiger tank may have thought that the Hellcat was completely knocked out and abandoned since the American tank destroyer had never moved or fired. For that matter, the Tiger tank may have been the weapon that had initially fired at the Hellcat.

Not long after the standoff began, an American soldier surprised Dayton when he whispered down from above. The fellow soldier hid behind the turret and nearby tree limbs to keep from being seen by the enemy, and the exposed and unprotected turret top of the Hellcat made it easier for him to communicate with Dayton.

The soldier explained he had been sent to see what was holding Dayton up. Along the way he'd also done some scouting of the enemy. The soldier informed Dayton there was a German Panther tank immediately to their right and sitting out in the open. He mentioned that along with the Panther 400 yards away, there appeared to be hundreds upon hundreds of German soldiers in the woods on each side of the road. The German soldiers were moving in and massing up.

Dayton was thankful for the recon on the Panther tank and German Infantry, since he had seen neither. He had been too focused, and rightly so, on the big barrel of the Royal King Tiger tank pointed directly at him. He readily admitted of never seeing the Panther or the German Infantry until the whispered messages from his surprise visitor.

Even before the other American arrived Dayton had already considered firing at the King Tiger. He felt he needed to do something and not just sit there. Once he knew there were more of the enemy than he first thought, he decided he really needed a loader to have any chance at success. Dayton asked the other soldier to come down and be his loader. He explained his plan to fire off a few rounds fast in an effort to damage the enemy. If they were unsuccessful, Dayton promised they'd high-tail it outta there. The other American responded by quietly telling Dayton, "I'm no-o-o-o-o-o-o-o-o tanker, and goo-o-o-o-o-o-o-o-od bye." With those final words, that soldier took off to the American lines!

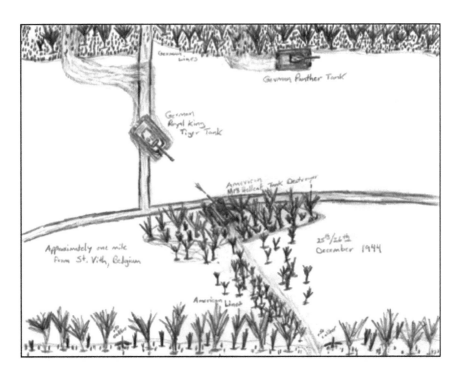

Battle scene as described by Dayton.

Above and Beyond

War is an ugly thing but not the ugliest of things. The decayed and degraded state of moral and patriotic feeling which thinks that nothing is worth war is much worse. The man who has nothing for which he is willing to fight and nothing that he cares more about than his personal safety is a miserable creature who has no chance of being free unless made and kept so by the exertions of better men than himself.

John S. Mill

Dayton did not blame or begrudge the other soldier for not sticking around. Matter of fact Dayton said, "That soldier was the smart one for leaving, and for a split second I almost went with him." Instead, he stayed, hoping to fire off at least a round or two.

Firm in his resolve to engage the enemy, Dayton considered what he should do first. Before knowing there was a Panther tank to his right, he had only focused on the big gun of the Tiger. If nothing else, maybe he could do some damage to the Tiger's main weapon. Disabling that gun might give him a ghost of a chance.

Dayton knew he would have to be perfect to succeed. If the first shot missed there probably wouldn't be a second opportunity before the Tiger fired back.

The news of a Panther to his right threw a real wrench in his plan of attack. Even though the Panther was over twice as far away as the Tiger, the Panther was still a much better target to aim for. The side of the Panther tank was exposed, which gave Dayton an excellent possibility of knocking out its tracks.

Plus the side armor on a Panther was only two inches thick and from short distances it was generally easy to penetrate. The Tiger tank, on the other hand, had only its frontal armor exposed as it faced directly at the Hellcat.

The frontal armor on a tank is its strongest point of defense. Dayton knew that taking on a Tiger head on was suicidal. The Tiger tank's barrel was already pointing at him and Dayton knew if he turned the turret towards the Panther, the Tiger would most likely blow him and the Hellcat to pieces. That option seemed more suicidal than taking on the Tiger head on. With really no choice other than running back to the American lines, Dayton made up his mind to fire at the Tiger. He said, "That barrel seemed like a big, hittable target."

Both German tanks stayed stationary which was unusual. Most enemy tanks would not stay out in the open without moving, especially so close to the American lines. It was either the 25th or 26th of December 1944 and was between two and three o'clock in the afternoon. Visibility was extremely limited due to the recent snowfall and low clouds in the area.

Dayton said, "Now that I was actually looking, I could see the Panther sitting still and the German Infantry moving into the woods." The Panther and infantry were both about 400 yards away. Most likely the infantry in the woods were massing up for a coordinated push against the American lines. With support from the two tanks the enemy infantry appeared to be planning an attack that evening, if not before, in which case Dayton would soon find his lap full of Germans.

If he was ever going to do something, now was the time, before the Germans got the jump on him. He adjusted the Hellcat's main weapon ever so slightly, hoping no one would notice the movement. The Tiger and Hellcat were level, and each had the other pretty well targeted. Dayton only needed to tighten up to make sure his aim was precise. He did his best to be smooth and quiet so the Germans didn't see or hear any activity from the Hellcat.

With his aim as good as it was going to get, Dayton squeezed off a single round at the Tiger tank's gun barrel. To his amazement, the turret exploded, flying into the air sending flames everywhere!

Dayton's high explosive shell hitting the 88mm cannon sent fragments and fire down the barrel, and based on the explosion of the Tiger tank's turret, those fragments must have hit an enemy round chambered and ready to be fired. In other words, the high explosive round essentially was similar to an oversized shotgun shell. Once it hit the gun, the entire round didn't have to go down the barrel to cause massive destruction. The shot did not have to be absolutely perfect. Just damn near!

Dayton had hit the barrel of a Tiger tank from over 150 yards away.

Leave it to a poor country boy from Kentucky who'd grown up in the Depression to make every shot count!

With success against the Tiger, Dayton turned the turret of the Hellcat to his right in the direction of the Panther. After quickly reloading, he fired one round and struck the tracks of the Panther disabling it. Dayton reloaded as fast as he could, and fired twice into the side and rear of the Panther tank. After taking three direct hits the Panther caught fire, eventually exploding. The Panther tank never moved or returned fire, not even small arms fire.

Once both enemy tanks were knocked out, Dayton continued reloading and firing as fast as possible, but now he directed his fire into the wooded areas to the right and left of the road some 400 yards away. The German infantry in those woods had been staging for an attack when he sent a barrage of high explosive rounds into their midst. Starting at the edge of the tree line to his right and using the Hellcat's 76 mm cannon, Dayton swept the enemy soldiers with fire from one end of the woods to the other.

As important as the high explosive shells were in Dayton's victory that day, they easily could have caused his own destruction. In order to succeed, he had to direct his own fire as loader and gunner combined. For him to load and fire as fast as possible, he was forced to place several live rounds on the floor of the Hellcat. It was extremely unconventional to have them out of their compartments and unprotected because, as the name implies, they were highly explosive. Each time a round was fired the hot spent shell casing was ejected, and often they would land in the part of the turret where Dayton was staging the live rounds. This put the staged rounds at risk of detonating from contact with the spent casings.

Dayton did what he called a "Hot Potato Dance" by kicking the hot empty shell casings away from the live shells, while at the same time continuing to fire on the enemy. Every time he fired the cannon of the Hellcat, he had to do this dance of loading, aiming, firing, and then kicking the hot spent shell casing away from the live rounds. He could only hope that none of those hot casings made contact with his staged ammo long enough to cause the Hellcat's turret to explode with him inside!

While he continued his "Hot Potato Dance," firing high explosive shells onto the enemy positions, the American soldiers behind him were doing well to hold their own. Some of the soldiers back on the line realized Dayton was engaging the enemy, because he said a couple of .50 calibers opened up to support him. Dayton continued firing at the wooded areas. His dance went on until, at some point, he could no longer see or hear any activity from any of the enemy positions.

The Professor and Stacker

The Germans were extremely successful at the onset of the Battle of the Bulge. However, American forces finally gained control and stopped the German offensive. They then began taking back territory lost during the initial enemy thrust. By the end of January 1945, most of Belgium was back under Allied control.

American forces suffered more casualties during the Battle of the Bulge than in any other battle of World War II. The Germans had spent their reserves to launch the attack, and even though the advance into Germany proved costly for Allied armies on both the Western and Eastern fronts, the German army had no chance of stopping them.

The day after Dayton engaged the enemy in the woods near St. Vith, American troops there moved forward to force the Germans back. The town of St. Vith itself was not recaptured until the 23rd January 1945.

General Bruce Clark and Lieutenant W.A. Knowlton talked to Dayton about his actions against the enemy. The two officers told him more than 450 German bodies had been found in the wooded areas where he had fired the high explosive shells. Dayton told the two officers to give credit for the high body count to the support he had received from the .50 caliber machine guns.

For his actions at the Battle of the Bulge, Pvt. Dayton Edie was recommended for the Medal of Honor and two Silver Star awards. General Bruce Clark nominated him for the Medal of Honor. Later, when General Patton arrived at the front, 'Old blood and guts' took over Dayton's paperwork, including his nomination for the Medal of Honor. The Medal of Honor is the highest award a soldier can receive and is awarded by the President in the name of the U. S. Congress. Dayton's bravery and extraordinary success at the Battle of the Bulge certainly made him worthy of the award.

Over the decades, both General Bruce Clark and Lieutenant Knowlton rose to prominence as four star Generals. General Knowlton would teach at the United States Military Academy at West Point.

When Allied soldiers arrived with trucks, they began transporting the German dead. Hundreds of dead enemy bodies had been carried out from the wooded areas, and Dayton watched as those corpses were literally stacked into the trucks.

Dayton Edie was a brave soldier fighting for a just cause but he never lost his humanity. After Dayton finished telling what he'd done at the Battle of the Bulge, tears streamed down his face. The last thing he said that night was, "So many fathers and sons."

The Medal of Honor Thrown Away

Having been nominated for the Medal of Honor, Dayton was introduced to Patton himself. Everything went fine until Patton noticed the shoulder patch on Dayton's uniform. Dayton was standing at attention and Patton spotted the Tank Destroyer patch. The patch seemed to infuriate Patton and the General said to Dayton, "So you're one of those cowards who let the Germans through at the Bulge."

The Tank Destroyer patch apparently made Patton think Dayton had been part of one of the green units overrun during the initial German attack. Dayton and the advance party of 30 soldiers did not arrive at the front until well after the initial attack and the breakthrough that followed. General Patton's disdain for Dayton probably had more to do with him being in the CIC rather than being a member of the Tank Destroyers.

> Aside from a few beach landings under enemy fire, most CIC agents' battles were against officers in their own Army.[6]

Regardless of the reason, Patton had just insulted a Medal of Honor nominee and accused him of cowardice.

Just before Dayton's confrontation with General Patton, a patrol had been sent out on reconnaissance in the early morning hours. The patrol had returned with no injuries or casualties. This was cause for celebration among the men, and evidently they were pretty loud in their whooping and hollering. Patton, who had just arrived at the front, went to see what the hoop-la was all about. He learned the celebration was a result of an entire patrol returning without injury. Patton barked that if nobody in the morning patrol got hurt, they hadn't done their jobs. He demanded that the patrol get back out there until somebody got hurt! An-

---

[6] Sayer and Botting, *America's Secret Army*, 28.

other patrol was then ordered out. On that patrol, one of the officers was killed.

Dayton, as a Signal Operating Instructions (SOI) operator, may have learned of Patton's order for another patrol to go back out resulting in an officer then getting killed, by hearing about it over the wire. It also may have just leaked out.

Knowing about the order to send the soldiers back out, Dayton spoke up. He mentioned the General's orders to stay on patrol until someone got hurt, and he questioned the legendary man. Dayton actually asked, "Why is it so important to lose lives at this stage of the battle?"

Patton was unaware his order had become known. Since Dayton was supposed to be standing at attention when he spoke up, his outburst was a severe breach of protocol, but to make things worse, a lowly private was questioning a General's orders. Patton was furious, especially with the small private standing before him.

The General began to unleash his anger upon the insubordinate private. Patton ordered Dayton to march to a tent where his makeshift office was set up, yelling and cursing at him the whole way there. Once in the office, Patton continued to curse, swear, and yell. The General defended his order saying that the soldiers who had gone out earlier that morning had not done their jobs. He kept saying those soldiers were nothing more than a bunch of "damn cowards!"

He said it was an embarrassment for any soldier to go out and not see action, not like those who had fought at the Battle of the Bulge!

Over and over again, General Patton yelled that those soldiers on patrol had been 'cowards for not facing the enemy, nothing but a bunch of damn cowards who were just trying to survive until the war ended, unlike those that had fought at the Bulge!'

Having heard enough, Dayton couldn't help himself and spoke out again. "At the Battle of the Bulge I saw and worked under Generals Clark, Hodges, Middleton, Jones, and Gavin, but I don't remember seeing you there."

Already insanely angry, Dayton's smart mouth sent Patton over the edge. Patton's response was like an active volcano spewing obscenities instead of lava. General Patton went around to the rear of Dayton as he stood at attention and kicked Dayton hard in his backside.

General Patton then went to his desk and pulled a stack of paperwork from one of the drawers. The General took that paperwork and tore parts of it up, threw all of it in a garbage can, and set the contents of the can on fire.

General Patton told Dayton what he had just done—that all his paperwork including his Medal of Honor nomination had literally gone up in smoke! The written details of Dayton Edie's actions against the enemy at the Battle of the Bulge and his nomination for the Medal of Honor were gone forever. The General then told Dayton he would never get the medals he had earned at the Battle of the Bulge, which proved to be quite true. The General further added that with all his paperwork gone it would be as if Dayton had never even been in the war.

At the time Dayton was less concerned with having lost his paperwork and medals than he was about a possible court martial for insubordination.

Once the smoke of Patton's eruptions cleared, some of Dayton's fellow soldiers managed to get him out of the tent and away from the infuriated General. It is likely those soldiers saved Dayton's career in the U.S. military.

Before learning about Dayton's run-in with General Patton, I had asked him why he hadn't been given the Congressional Medal of Honor for his actions at the Battle of the Bulge. Dayton only said, "People get angry and jealous and tear up paperwork."

Dayton once said it was probably for the best that he hadn't received the Medal of Honor. He felt that many who had earned the coveted medal had lived short and sometimes rough lives. Dayton said many became alcoholics as they tried to forget the horrors of war, but never able to fully put it behind them.

The image above is from the *History of the 605th T.D. Battalion 1941-1945*, Lt. Col. D. F. Buchwald, Commanding. This map is the route the 605th and Dayton took through Europe.

Cover of the *History of the 605th T.D. Battalion 1941-1945.*

Members of the 605th Tank Destroyer Battalion. Dayton is in front row at left.

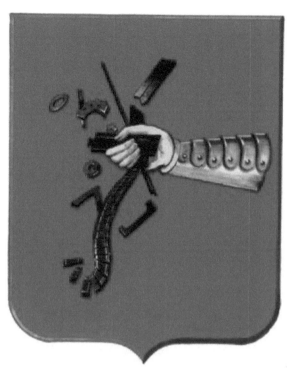

COAT OF ARMS FOR STANDARD OF
605th TANK DESTROYER BATTALION
FULL SIZE
REFERENCE: Q.M. DRAWING NO. 5-6-865

Capture and Escape

Shortly after Dayton's confrontation with General Patton, he was captured and taken prisoner. He told me about it only once, saying "It was the most embarrassing time of my life. With the training I had, it never should have happened." Dayton had reason to make that statement.

As early as August 1944 the CIC headquarter detachments had begun to issue warnings about the danger posed by German soldiers masquerading as American soldiers by dressing themselves in bits and pieces of American uniforms taken from dead or captured Americans and driving about the front in captured US Army jeeps.[7]

On the day Dayton was captured he was sitting in a foxhole, rifle in hand, when a jeep came by with a couple of U. S. soldiers inside. The two Americans asked him if he wanted something hot to eat. Dayton said no, but he thanked them and never put down his rifle.

Later, the jeep came back again, and again the soldiers asked if he wanted some food. This time he was persuaded. He put his gun down, and climbed out of his foxhole. Unfortunately, the two friendly Americans turned out to be German soldiers disguised as Americans. With Dayton disarmed, they easily overpowered him and took him prisoner. Apparently, the jeep with the two Krauts parading as GIs had gone around collecting prisoners all day, and had gathered quite a haul all without firing a shot.

Dayton and some other POWs were being held together when a German soldier came along and noticed Dayton's boots. The German decided he wanted those boots, so he ordered Dayton to remove them and hand them over. This left Dayton in the awkward circumstance of standing in the snow in his stocking feet. Before he could get replacements, German soldiers and prisoners were ordered to the German border. The other POWs were taken

---

[7] Sayer and Botting, *America's Secret Army*, 176.

away as an old German soldier looked around trying to find something for Dayton's feet.

Dayton said, "The American artillery had finally woken up!"

As darkness began to fall, an artillery barrage came in with shells landing near where shoeless Dayton was standing in the cold. Those who had not left either hit the ground or ran toward the German border. During the chaos Dayton attacked the nearest German soldier from behind, snapping his neck killing him instantly. By this time an older and slower German tried to quickly unsling his rifle, but fumbled getting it off his shoulder.

Taking a knife from the belt of the German he had just killed, Dayton charged at the old German soldier. The old German had finally unslung his rifle, but before he could raise the weapon to fire Dayton lunged stabbing him with the knife quickly taking the old German to the ground. The old German had been the one looking for shoes to replace Dayton's commandeered boots. The man was wounded, but he was not dead.

Realizing he was now free, Dayton refused to leave the injured man behind and decided to take him along in search of the American lines. Despite the fact Dayton had caused his injury, the old German was grateful to go with him.

Dayton and his German prisoner stayed low to the ground as they started crawling through the snow.

Dayton tended the old German's wounds, as best he could, while they hid out for a short time in a barn. They used the barn for shelter until the farmer came along and discovered them. When the farmer ran off, they feared he would run to the Germans and tell them where they were. It was decided to leave the warmth and protection of the barn.

When the other Germans pulled back, a young Kraut signalman had been left behind. He climbed a tree out of fear. Up in that tree, the young German spotted Dayton and his wounded German prisoner crawling through the snow. The younger man saw Dayton helping the wounded soldier and decided not to shoot the American. Instead, he climbed down the tree and gave himself up. Dayton now had two prisoners. He always laughed at this because he said both men only wanted, as did he, to get to the safety of American lines.

After almost a week with no food and now without shelter, they were all getting weak. Dayton knew they had to do something or they were not going to survive. Using some wire that belonged to the young signalman, he tied all three of them together. Dayton and the younger German crawled along, dragging the wounded man behind. Dayton kept the cold, wet, hungry trio always headed in the direction of American artillery fire. The three made their way through the snow, Dayton still without shoes, hoping always to get back to his comrades.

After the three had crawled near the American lines, Dayton weakly raised his arm and yelled, "I'm an American!"

Fortunately, the three of them were close enough that American soldiers heard Dayton and came to their aid. After a week without food Dayton was as thin as a rail.

Dayton learned that night the old German soldier had died. He never saw the young German signalman again and he never found out what happened to him. This always bothered Dayton since the boy was so crucial in getting them safely back. Without help from the young German they never would have made it.

For days he had worked so hard to keep the man he had wounded alive. It was devastating to know the old German had died the very night they managed to find help.

Dayton himself was down to nothing but skin and bones. It took three weeks for him to fully recover and return to action.

Fighting in a Churchill

After Dayton's escape and subsequent recovery, he spent eleven days fighting alongside the British. He was in the British Zone which was under the Command of Field Marshal Montgomery. After spending weeks recovering from malnutrition, there were no American units nearby for him to join when he returned to active duty. Because of his gunnery skills, Dayton was asked to tag along with the British in a Churchill tank. They were in Luneberg, Germany, near Hannover.

The British Churchill tanks were commanded by Major Clark. Dayton only ever referred to him by his rank and last name. However, based on records from that time, it was probably Major James Henry Mullin Clark. Dayton said Major Clark was a pro at spotting and directing fire. As a commander in the field Dayton said, "He was one of the best I'd ever seen, and a natural tanker."

The Churchill tanks had been assigned the task of knocking out enemy anti-tank emplacements. The anti-tank emplacements, or pillboxes as they were called, and their guns were dug in with concrete all around. There was a slit or opening in the front to allow guns to fire at the enemy. The defense on the flanks and to the rear had been overrun, leaving these pillboxes on their own and defenseless from a rear or side attack. While the British worked methodically to knock out the pillboxes, one of them continued to doggedly avoid destruction.

The British tank gunners kept bouncing shells off this particular pillbox to no avail. Dayton spoke up and asked if he could take a shot at the stubborn pillbox.

Major Clark liked the marksmanship of the American private and was the officer who had made him a gunner inside one of the Churchill tanks. The Major gave Dayton permission to take a shot at this seemingly indestructible enemy pillbox. Clark personally agreed to direct his fire.

Dayton took aim directly at the slit of the pillbox. With Major Clark's guidance, he aimed and fired. The round missed the slit and ricocheted off the pillbox just as all the other previous shells had.

After reloading, Dayton aimed again. With the Major directing him again, he fired off a round. His second shot went perfectly into the slit of the pillbox causing the entire emplacement to explode into pieces.

It's a well-known truth the British love their tea, but Dayton always felt it was more than love; it was a necessity. At certain times of the day while he was attached to the Brits, all activity stopped for tea breaks. Dayton waited nervously during these tea breaks while sitting in the stationary Churchill. He was uneasy because a stationary tank made a wonderful target. He was especially concerned since he had already taught the Germans a deadly lesson about what could happen when a tank sits still too long. Fortunately his tank was never targeted while his British chums enjoyed a spot of tea. Though the issue with mandatory tea time almost gave him an ulcer, Dayton really enjoyed the time spent fighting alongside the British. Sometime in February 1945 Dayton rejoined the 605th Tank Destroyer Battalion.

On a military financial document, there is a record of every month he was paid from 16th March 1943, to 27th April 1946. On that record next to the months of January and February 1945 the document, shown on next two pages, says 'foreign,' which indicates the time he spent with the British.

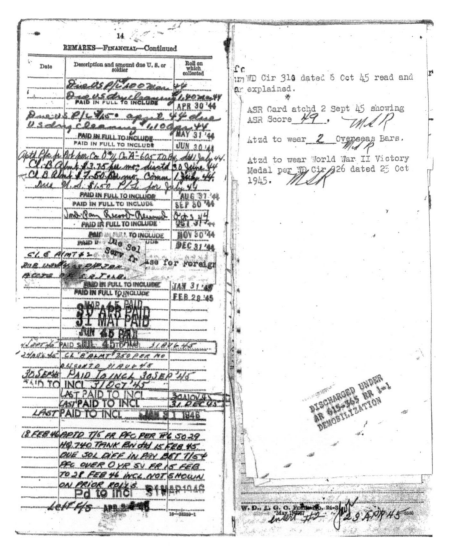

Financial Service Records, May 1944–April 1946.

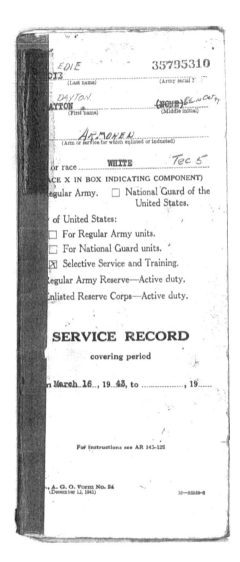

Financial Service Records, May 1944-April 1946.

Close Calls and Bridges

Near the Roer River, Dayton watched once as a German plane crashed not far from his location. The enemy plane had been shot down close to his position, but it landed on the opposite side of the river. Always curious, Dayton requested permission to work his way over to the crashed plane. On the other side of the river and close to the crash, he spotted three Germans running in and out of the burning plane.

With the plane on fire, it seemed the soldiers were rushing back and forth to rescue other members of their crew. Dayton had been trained to strike the hardest target first, with all other targets following in order of difficulty. This approach gave a man a better chance to take out all targets, hopefully before any could fire back.

Dayton tried to site the German soldiers in line, and was just about to squeeze the trigger when one of the three moved out of the line of fire. This happened three or four times when he was very close to firing. However, he was never able to line them up long enough, so he was never able to shoot. He decided to move closer to the targets so he could finally get all three in line long enough to shoot.

As he moved in for the kill, he ran into an American lieutenant who stopped him and asked if he was headed to the crashed plane. He confirmed, yes, he was, and the lieutenant informed Dayton he already had three guys at the crash site examining the wreckage. The officer finished by telling him not to worry about the plane. He had it all under control.

Dayton left, never telling the Lieutenant how close he was to not having those three soldiers. Having nearly killed fellow American soldiers caused Dayton a lot of sleepless nights. He never forgot that incident.

With Allied forces on the offensive, the Germans were pushed back to the Rhine River. At the German town of Krefeld, after having a tough time taking the surrounding area, American forces took the town itself when the Germans pulled out on the 3rd of March 1945. As part of the attacking force that had taken Krefeld, Dayton was in a recon Platoon from the 605th Tank Destroyer Battalion while attached to the 405th Infantry Regiment. The 405th Infantry Regiment was heavily involved in Krefeld's capture.

After surrendering Krefeld, the Germans left their flag still flying in the town square. The rope it was on had been cut, and since the Germans had left Krefeld in such a hurry they had not been able to retrieve their flag.

The German flag was flying 30 feet in the air and was attached to a rusty iron pole. Two or three Americans tried to climb the pole to cut down the offending flag. None of them could get higher than 10 feet up the pole when they came sliding back down. Dayton decided to see if he could do any better than his buddies. He started up the pole, creeping up four to six inches at a time. Moving in small increments like that took a while, but eventually he made it to the top. It was a large flag that was much larger than Dayton. Hanging onto that rusty pole, 30 feet in the air, Dayton pulled out his trench knife and cut the German flag loose. Then, with the flag draped around him, he carefully slid back down the pole where the others waited. Many of those men proceeded to write their names on the surrendered German flag.

Of course, everyone celebrated and clapped Dayton on the back for a job well done. Only then did he realize how dumb he had been to climb that pole. If there had been an enemy sniper in the area, it would have been an easy task for him to take Dayton out. Especially since the Germans probably weren't too happy about the Americans cutting down their flag.

A few days later Dayton again was detached from the 605th T.D. Battalion.

This time his assignment was guard duty at the Remagen Bridge. The Bridge had been taken on the 7th March 1945. During his assignment to guard the bridge he was attached to the 79th Infantry division.

While guarding the bridge, Dayton was not part of a tank crew. Instead Dayton had his own jeep. The jeep was equipped with two Browning machine guns, consisting of a mounted .50 caliber and an unattached .30 caliber. A private with his own heavily armed jeep, guarding the Remagen Bridge—a high priority target, all point clearly to his position with the CIC.

Word came that German Underwater Demolition Teams (UDT) had been sent to attack the Remagen Bridge. It was believed the enemy Frogmen would swim down the Rhine River along the east bank to reach the bridge, and once there they would place demolitions to destroy the important structure.

Dayton had orders to go down to the river's edge that evening at dark. Being an expert machine gunner, he was given orders to spray machine gun fire into the river and along the east bank. His exact orders were to continue firing until he was out of ammo. More ammo would be brought long before there was ever a chance of him running out. Dayton said years later, "Evidently, they didn't know how fast I could fire a machine gun, because I ran out of ammo way before anyone arrived with more!"

This preemptive strike to secure the bridge occurred on the second day of his assignment at Remagen Bridge. No one at the bridge ever reported seeing any German UDTs. There were German Frogmen sent to demolish the bridge but, apparently, they were killed before reaching their objective. Dayton and others guarded the bridge for five or six days until their orders were changed. At no time did Dayton himself cross the Remagen Bridge to the east side of the Rhine, and he was ordered elsewhere before its collapse.

The names of the men who saw Dayton cut it down are written on the enemy flag taken from Krefeld. One of the above names is Sgt. Lynn. His grandson, Matthew Lynn, created a web site to honor the men of the 605th Tank Destroyer Battalion, and was given the flag by Marta Edie.

Twice Wounded

Dayton was assigned to his primary unit, the 605th Tank Destroyer Battalion, when they crossed the Rhine River at noon on Palm Sunday. On Easter Sunday, while near Munster, Germany, Padre Sgt. Elwood sang The Old Rugged Cross.

Dayton again left the 605th Tank Destroyer Battalion after being ordered attached to the 82nd Airborne Division. During his career in the U.S. Army he broke off from one unit and attached to another on numerous occasions. This constant movement from one unit to another resulted in Dayton having been attached to every U.S. Army in the European theater during World War II except the Fifth Army in Italy.

Sometime around the 28th March 1945, in less than 24 hours Dayton was wounded twice, both times just outside Dulmen, Germany. The first time he was wounded it happened to his right foot, which had been badly frostbitten during the Battle of the Bulge.

An enemy shell had landed nearby sending a piece of shrapnel through his boot and slicing off the bottom of Dayton's big toe. Even decades later he said that toe nail still fell off on occasion, but it always grew back.

Less than 24 hours later, he was wounded again. Dayton was trying to get around a German flak gun when an enemy machine gun opened up sending a line of bullets right at him. A round grazed the bottom of his chin. He believed he was spared a direct hit to either his face or chest because of his outstanding training. Back at Camp Hood all the new recruits had been trained to zigzag when crossing open ground. By zigzagging soldiers never exposed the broad part of the body - the largest target - in the same position but for a second. He was absolutely positive, that if he had not zigzagged, he would have been killed or seriously wounded by the round that grazed his chin.

The area in and around Dulmen, Germany was heavily fortified. General Rose was killed in that same area two days after Dayton himself had been wounded there twice. Maj. General

Maurice Rose of the 3rd Armored Division was killed while moving forward with the troops on the 30th March 1945. He is buried at the American Cemetery in Margraten, The Netherlands.

There is no official paperwork or Purple Heart Medal for Dayton's wounds at Dulmen.

Generals Disobeying Orders

The war was coming to an end, and Germany was down to its last reserves. In many cases this meant young boys and elderly men well past their prime. The remnants of the German Army were being crushed by Allied forces. As the American and British Armies drove east, the enormous Russian Army pushed west, until it breached the German frontier itself.

On the Eastern front, German soldiers usually had to fight to their death.

There was no mercy from the Russians. The Russians still remembered when the Germans attacked in 1941 and had shown little mercy to either Russian soldiers or civilians. When the German attack started after years of brutal dictatorship under Stalin, many Russian civilians had opened their arms willingly to their enemy.

Much to their surprise, the Germans showed as little mercy to civilians as they did to Russian soldiers in battle. The situation grew even worse when SS Troops arrived to round up all Jews, Gypsies, gays, and others of 'undesirable' races and groups.

By 1945, almost four years after Germany had attacked the Kremlin, the Russian Armies were now pushing into Germany and they were ready for payback. In the east, German civilians fled to escape the oncoming Russian forces. With the German soldiers unable to hold the Red Armies back, many Russian soldiers exacted revenge on their enemy, killing, brutalizing, and raping untold numbers of German civilians in the final months of the war. Historians estimate that millions of German women were raped by Russian soldiers during those tragic months.

As the Russians pushed west, U.S. and British forces reached the Elbe River with orders not to cross it under any circumstances. On the other side of the Elbe River was territory that had been put under Russian control. The orders not to cross the Elbe River had come directly from Supreme Allied Commander General Dwight D. Eisenhower. General Eisenhower's exact orders were for all units to stay on their designated side of the Elbe River and destroy any German forces trying to cross it.

The problem with those orders was information had started trickling in that hundreds of Allied POWs were on the other side of the river. Dayton had been assigned to the 82nd Airborne Division as the Signal Operating Instructions (SOI) operator for General Gavin, Commander of the division. Even after the information about captured American and British soldiers was sent to him twice, General Eisenhower still refused to change his orders and allow U.S. forces to cross the river and rescue the prisoners.

Dayton, as the SOI operator for the division was receiving, decoding, and sending all the orders and communications between several generals, including those from Eisenhower. The 82nd Airborne Division commander, General James Gavin, and Lieutenant Colonel George Kenneth Rubel, Commander of the 740th Tank Battalion were the two officers Dayton respected and spoke of most often.

General Gavin was known to say the 740th Tank Battalion, under the command of Colonel Rubel, was one of the few units that could keep up with his 82nd Airborne Division. The 740th Tank Battalion was thus given the honor of wearing the 82nd Airborne Division shoulder patch.

Trusted information had been received about Allied prisoners on the other side of the Elbe River. Even so, three generals had been ordered at least twice not to cross the river. Eventually, the Russians were expected to push the Germans westward all the way to the Elbe, crushing them up against the river and the American forces on the other side. Anything or anyone caught on the wrong side of the river could end up being crushed against it. The Allied generals seriously feared the Germans would eventually execute all their prisoners before the Russians arrived. Convinced that Allied prisoners were in danger, General Gavin decided to defy a direct order and take his division across the Elbe River.

The official reasons these divisions crossed the Elbe are far different from what you see here. But being the SOI operator for General Gavin, Dayton had firsthand knowledge of all communications and always professed the initial and primary reason the three American divisions, along with British forces had crossed the Elbe River was only to save Allied POWs.

The two other generals pushing General Eisenhower for permission to cross the Elbe River were General Bryant E. Moore, 8th

Infantry Division, and General Isaac D. White, 2nd Armored Division.

General Gavin at age 36 during World War II, was the youngest general in the U.S. Army to command a division. General Gavin was pushing the hardest to cross the Elbe River, because he was more concerned with saving American lives than he was with winning favor with Eisenhower. You can understand why Dayton admired and respected him so much. All three Generals, however, suffered a great deal over their decision whether or not to disregard a direct order and save the Allied prisoners.

Dayton said many times the situation became extremely emotional. They hated having their hands tied when it came to saving America's fighting men.

General Gavin was set to take the 82nd Airborne Division across the river, orders or not, but British Field Marshal Montgomery learned of the plan and sent orders to General Gavin saying, "I'm in charge here!"

Technically the Field Marshal was right. He had command over all Allied forces in the area. Even though they were American, the three divisions were under his command. Then, much to the surprise of General Gavin and the other two generals, Montgomery told them he agreed with the information they had received and ordered them to cross the river in search of Allied prisoners. The three Generals now had direct orders to cross the Elbe River from Field Marshal Montgomery, while at the same time having direct orders from Supreme Allied Commander General Eisenhower not to cross. The three Generals decided to cross, but in order to try to convince General Eisenhower otherwise, a regiment from each of the three divisions were set with the right radio frequencies and left on the American side of the Elbe River.

After crossing the river Dayton went from being General Gavin's SOI operator to working security for General Moore. This decision by General Gavin to defy Eisenhower's direct order greatly hindered Gavin's career advancement after the war. All three Generals had risked court martial by disobeying direct orders from General Eisenhower.

The three American divisions crossed the Elbe River so swiftly they caught the Germans completely off guard. Allied forces quickly overtook all opposition on the other side of the river. In most cases, German forces were more than happy to surrender rather than face the probability of death against the Russians. Only 50 miles on the other side of the river, more than 800 American and British POWs were freed from German captors!

The same 740th Tank Battalion which had stopped the Germans during the Battle of the Bulge at Stoumont, and later forced S.S. Colonel Peiper's men to abandon their tanks at La Gleize, suddenly became part of the force crossing the Elbe River.

Colonel Rubel, Commander of the 740th Tank Battalion said, "My plan had been to follow the spearhead tank to keep the column moving as fast as possible, and if anything should come up, I could handle it instantly. The plan worked well until we came to the town of Gramitz, where we liberated about 400 American prisoners of war, and an equal number of British, not to mention 2,000 or 3,000 French, Italians, and Poles who had been doing forced labor there."[8]

The quote confirms that along with the 800 Allied prisoners, there were also 2,000 to 3,000 European slave laborers who would have perished if not for the courage of those generals who defied direct orders. During the two week period that American and British forces were on the Russian side of the river, between one and two million Germans were able to cross the Elbe to flee the oncoming Russians. These refugees surely owed their lives or at the least their freedom to the courage and strength of three brave American generals.

---

[8] Rubel, *Daredevil Tankers*, 216, 217.

Nazis

The three American divisions made their foray across the Elbe River with such ease that they continued in search of Allied POWs, pushing off to the northeast. Dayton was assigned the task of escorting General Moore as one of his personal bodyguards, all in a fast moving armored column. Dayton was the tail gunner in the rear vehicle of the armored column. They were moving along at a fast pace when Dayton noticed what looked like barbed wire, possibly a prisoner of war camp on one side of the road. Being in the rear of the column, Dayton radioed his driver to stop while he and another soldier went to investigate. Finding the gate unlocked, the two men readied their weapons and slipped inside. They expected fully armed guards and additional prisoners of war, and they wanted to catch any remaining Germans unprepared.

Walking into Wobbelin the two American soldiers did find more prisoners. But these were not Allied POWs, nor was this a normal prisoner of war camp. It was something neither of the American soldiers could have imagined in their worst nightmares — a concentration camp.

Dayton and the other American soldier found dead bodies everywhere, and many of the living prisoners were barely alive. Those living were so weak they had remained in the camp even though the gates were unlocked. Many had no place else to go.

One of the first people they saw was a little lady with her bike. Dayton took a picture of her clinging to her meager possessions. She passed them as she walked weakly to the gate. They asked her where the Germans were and she told Dayton they were gone. All gone.

There were a number of buildings in the camp, all made of brick as lumber was difficult to find in this northern region. Dayton learned later that the prisoners had been forced by the Nazis to build not only the buildings but the ovens. It is uncertain if the ovens at Wobbelin were ever put to use, as fuel had become difficult to requisition this late in the war, but the S.S. had personally overseen the building and management of Wobbelin. The prisoners had also been forced to dig the pits—numerous pits 12 feet deep by 15 feet wide where the dead and dying were thrown until the bodies could be transported from the camp.

The two American soldiers looked inside the nearest building and were convinced everyone was dead. After seeing only a little of the horrible camp, Dayton and the other soldier somberly returned to their vehicle and caught up with the armored column. Dayton radioed about the camp and its location to the 82nd Airborne Division HQ.

Once Dayton was back with his armored column, he talked to his commander about the camp and of going back to help those abandoned there. His commander refused to return, reminding Dayton the 82nd Airborne Division had been tasked to help the camp and its survivors. Dayton didn't know why, but he felt compelled to return. He asked his good friend, Tex Baker to drive him back to Wobbelin. Tex had access to a jeep, and Dayton figured they could get there and back without being missed. Seeing Dayton was clearly upset, Tex asked, "What's wrong Ken-tuck?" (Put the accent on the first syllable.) Dayton told him it was just something he'd seen without going into detail about the camp.

Upon arriving at Wobbelin Dayton took Tex and together they made a full reconnoiter of the concentration camp. Afterwards and even though it was his jeep, Tex was so upset by what he saw inside the camp that Dayton had to drive them back to their outfit.

Near the end of the war, Wobbelin had been built to hold concentration camp inmates whose camps were being overrun by Allied forces. Survivors of Wobbelin say it was actually the worst of the camps. Wobbelin was not set up like extermination camps to gas people or kill them off through slave labor, but instead it was a camp of last resort. The Nazis were trying to exterminate as many witnesses as possible. At Wobbelin there was little food or water, and the only thing the prisoners did was take part in never ending roll calls where they were forced to stand for hours at a time. The Nazis put prisoners in Wobbelin to starve them to death!

When the GIs liberated the concentration camp at Wobbelin, Dayton said they discovered and freed survivors from many nationalities. One survivor included an American who had been held in Germany since the attack on Pearl Harbor.

The American was trapped there when Hitler declared war on the United States shortly after the attack on Pearl Harbor. The man had refused to aid the Germans, and for years the Gestapo had made him suffer for not cooperating.

Since late 1941, the American had barely managed to survive, until finally ending up at Wobbelin sometime after the camp opened in February 1945.

Allied forces learned Germans had used the railroad near Wobbelin to dispose of dead bodies in the Baltic Sea. The Nazis sent any corpses from other nearby camps or from Wobbelin to the Baltic coast by train, where they then were loaded onto ships. Filled with corpses, the ships were taken just off shore and sunk. The Germans were trying to hide their atrocities by sinking the ships to the bottom of the Baltic Sea. British planes, however, knocked out the trains and the railroad tracks before all the bodies could be transported.

Some of the corpses on those trains actually turned out to be living people who had escaped by playing dead. They had not only lived through the horrors of the camp and being hauled by train among the dead bodies and loaded on to the ships, but then they had survived being sunk. A few of these poor individuals somehow managed to swim to shore and lived to testify later against their former captors.

Dayton estimated they found 2000-3000 dead bodies inside the camp and about 2000 survivors. Army Chaplin George Woods was summoned and gave last rites to all the dead and dying and attempted to say a prayer from the proper religion for each prisoner.

After the survivors were removed, but before the bodies were interred German men and women over 18 were brought to the camp so the German population could see the horror their countrymen had perpetuated there. Bodies were found in every building, and the American Army forced local Germans to help move and bury the dead. This policy was instated to ensure the Germans never forgot what had been done. After the camp was empty, all buildings but one were razed. That last building became a Remembrance Museum and fell behind the Iron Curtain shortly after the end of the war.

Back in 1945 and during the short amount of time he was there, Dayton befriended a survivor at Wobbelin the same age as he. The young man's name was Erich Kary, and he was Jewish. Erich had lost his entire family at Auschwitz; his mother, father, and two sisters. Erich had been spared because he was skilled as a carpenter. At one point he was forced to help build skids to launch V-1 rockets—buzz bombs.

Years later, when East and West Germany reunited, an annual reunion was started for the liberators of the camp along with those who had survived Wobbelin. It was held on May 2nd, the anniversary of the date the camp was liberated. At the first reunion, Dayton and Erich met again and rekindled a very special friendship.

Wobbelin.

Wobbelin.

Wobbelin.

Wobbelin.

Wobbelin.

The General's Favorite Stable Boy

Fortunately for them, Generals Gavin, Moore, and White were not court-martialed for disobeying direct orders. It seems British Field Marshal Montgomery and Supreme Allied Commander General Eisenhower didn't care much for each other, and Montgomery wasn't about to pass up any opportunity to countermand an order given by Eisenhower. Field Marshal Montgomery exonerated the American Generals by taking full responsibility for the crossing of the Elbe River.

The three Generals had done what was needed, and by crossing the Elbe they had saved untold numbers of lives. The ruse of having the three divisional regiments stay behind had fooled General Eisenhower for 10 to 11 days. The three divisions, including British forces, stayed on the Russian side of the Elbe River for about 14 days. Dayton said one night they received orders to get back to the Allied side of the river. The orders came in around midnight, and by the next morning everyone had crossed the Elbe back to the Allied designated side, mostly using a pontoon bridge over the river. The bridge was named the Harry S. Truman.

Shortly after the incident at the Elbe further south in Austria, the famous Lipizzaner stallions were in danger of being eaten by starving locals. To save the horses, General Patton made the stallions and the Spanish Riding School which owned them wards of the U.S. Army. Wanting to see the stallions himself, Dayton worked his way down to Austria. Dayton pretended he had a brother heading stateside to get permission to leave his unit.

With his Dad having married 10 times, Dayton may have had a half- brother or two out there, but according to him he had none. In order to obtain leaves to 'sightsee' on occasion, Dayton told his superior officers he had a brother in the service who was about to be shipped out. The need to visit a phantom brother on occasion gave him more freedom to move about.

Members of the Counter Intelligence Corp (CIC) including Dayton were authorized to travel just about anywhere they wanted, compared to normal non-commissioned officers.

At times they enjoyed extraordinary power far beyond the normal expectations of their rank and status, and a freedom of movement and right of access which could be alarming to the conventional regimental mind.[9]

Dayton had no idea that Patton had remained with the horses for a time. Patton had met the Master of the Spanish Riding School, Alois Podhajsky, during the 1912 Olympics and agreed to hear his concerns about the famed stallions. Dayton actually admired Patton for his military tactics, but what bothered him was how Patton always seemed to believe blood had to be shed for troops to be successful. He had certainly not forgotten his first encounter with 'Old Blood and Guts' nearly six months earlier. His adventures since then, including capture, escape, fighting across Germany, and discovering the horrors of a concentration camp, were all a memory now.

The truth he had discovered at Wobbelin had been hard to take, and Dayton needed some downtime. He worked his way into Austria where the beautiful horses were being protected by the U.S. Army.

Dayton managed to get a job in the stables, probably because of his extensive equestrian experience prior to the war. He had worked a two-horse team on his father's farm near Carntown. Being so good with horses, he not only finagled his way into the stable, he was able eventually to join the stable crew. That is when, to his shock and dismay, Dayton learned Patton came to the stables daily to ride one of the famed Lipizzaner stallions.

Oddly, General Patton never recognized Dayton from their first encounter.

It is difficult to believe, but by the end of the war Patton did not remember or recognize the young private he had berated so fiercely at the Battle of the Bulge.

---

[9] Sayer and Botting, *America's Secret Army*, 4

Decades later, Dayton honestly believed General Patton had probably been suffering with Alzheimer's toward the end of his life.

Even more shocking than the fact Patton had completely forgotten Dayton was the fact he made Dayton his favorite stable boy. In the space of six months, his relationship with General Patton went from losing his nomination for the Medal of Honor and almost being court-martialed to suddenly becoming his favorite stable boy. Patton ended up loving Dayton and literally treating him like a son, offering him other plum assignments besides that of personal stable boy. Patton told Dayton he could be his personal body guard or his driver. Dayton turned down every assignment offered.

On one occasion, when he was trying to talk Dayton into taking one of these plum assignments, Patton ordered Dayton to sit on his lap. Patton seemed to think the arrangement would convey his sincere affection for Dayton. It did nothing but make Dayton extremely uncomfortable.

While Patton did not remember Dayton, Dayton still remembered the entire encounter with the General following the Battle of the Bulge. He hadn't forgotten, nor had he forgiven. It became a daily ritual with Dayton to try to pull off a small prank to get even with the famous man. After gaining enough favor to be personally saddling the General's stallion each day, he tried to rig the saddle to loosen and slip during the ride. The goal was to have Patton fall from his horse and be humbled a bit. Dayton wanted to get even for the brave men he felt Patton had dishonored with his comments in Belgium, and he was not above holding a grudge for the loss of the medals Patton had thrown away.

It was fortunate Dayton was never able to succeed with his prank. Every time he set the saddle so it would slip during the general's ride, the old Austrian in charge of the stable would come behind him to tighten things up just before Patton mounted the horse. After the old Austrian found the saddle loose a few mornings in a row, he figured out what Dayton was up to. He spoke to Dayton and told him he had to stop trying to rig General Patton's saddle. Dayton knew the Austrian was right, and he decided to hightail it out of there before his prank got him into real trouble.

In December of 1945, while in Germany, Patton's car was hit by another vehicle. The impact was not horrible, but it caught the

General off guard and left him with a broken neck. The General suffered terribly, paralyzed and lying on his back. General Patton lived in agonizing pain for twelve days and finally succumbed to blood clots on December 21, 1945.

WHITE HORSE TEAM
Old Guard Receives 10 Lipizzan Stallions

By JIM TICE
Times Staff Writer

FORT MYER, Va. — Ten Lipizzan stallions representing a breed of horse with some 400 years of military tradition have been donated to the Caisson Platoon of the 3d Inf (The Old Guard) by Tempel Farms of Niles, Ill.

Army Secretary John O. Marsh Jr., accepted the graceful high-strutting animals during a ceremony here that featured the Fife and Drum Corps, the Commander-in-Chief's Guard, the Caisson Platoon and B Co of The Old Guard. Tempel Smith Jr., president of Tempel Steel Co., represented Tempel Farms.

The Lipizzans will be used primarily by the Caisson Platoon to make up a "white horse team" for military funerals in Arlington National Cemetery and state funerals such as those held for Presidents Kennedy, Hoover and Eisenhower, and Generals MacArthur and Bradley. The unit also participates in retirement and wedding ceremonies here involving a brougham coach "Tally Ho" wagon, and an 18th century "marriage carriage."

The Tempel Farms collection of Lipizzans, consisting of more than 400 stallions, mares, colts and fillies, is the largest group of privately owned Lipizzans in the world. The breed, known for its strength, intelligence and grace, originated in Imperial Austria during the late 16th century when the Royal Court imported Spanish horses in an effort to improve its domestic breeds. The world-famous Spanish Riding School in Vienna was named for those horses.

Lipizzans and the Spanish Riding School also are a part of U.S. Army history.

When Allied and Soviet armies pushed into central Europe during the spring of 1945, the Spanish school's herd of Lipizzans was in danger of being destroyed, not only from bullets and bombs, but from a near-starving population who looked on the horses as a supply of fresh meat. Upon hearing of the danger from the school's commander, Gen. George S. Patton Jr., an old cavalryman with an avid appreciation for Lipizzans, made the sleek white horses wards of the Army.

When conditions were safe, Patton returned the Lipizzans to Vienna. The 10 horses recently donated to the Caisson Platoon are descended from that herd.

Gen. George S. Patton is shown in this August 1945, photo riding "Favory Africa," a Lipizzan that Adolph Hitler personally had selected as a gift for Emperor Hirohito of Japan. Patton's drive into Austria as the CG of Third Army prevented the gift from reaching the Emperor. The horse, which had belonged to the Spanish Riding School before being confiscated by the Germans, was returned to Vienna by Patton.

General Patton riding a stallion.

Boots and Amputation Orders

At night when German tankers were near, Dayton could hear their boots clanging against the tanks. With the enemy tank engines not running, the stillness of the night made that distinctive sound carry. The metal on the bottom of German boots hitting a tank was a sound every GI knew, and Dayton said it was not one they wanted to hear.

When the Battle of the Bulge was over in late January 1945, many GIs ended up with varying levels of frostbite. Most of the frostbite affected their feet, hands, and face. Before being captured, Dayton had a very nice pair of boots that he really liked. Unfortunately, a German soldier commandeered them before Dayton escaped.

While behind enemy lines and after a week in the snow and cold without boots, Dayton's feet were badly frostbitten. Dayton babied them while he convalesced and regained weight. After three weeks, he felt healthy enough to return to active duty and thought no more about his feet.

Later in the summer of 1945, his feet began bothering him again. The right foot hurt the worst, so in June of that year he went to see an Army doctor. After the doctor examined Dayton's feet, he ordered him to report back in two days. Then the doctor told Dayton something that guaranteed he would not report back to him as ordered. The doctor had told him, "Come back in two days. If that right foot doesn't get any better it will have to be amputated."

The two days came and went, and his right foot had not gotten any better. He endured a great deal of pain, but it was not so bad Dayton would allow it to be cut off!

During the war era there was no such thing as a second opinion. Refusing medical attention from an army doctor was grounds for a court-martial, so with the help of his sergeant and fellow soldiers, Dayton hid to avoid amputation. The other soldiers brought him food and allowed him to lay low, just in case the doctor came searching for his missing patient.

Sure enough, after the two days, the doctor went looking for Dayton.

Dayton's sergeant stepped up and convinced the doctor that the missing private had been sent to deliver tanks to the French. The sergeant told the doctor he had no idea when Dayton might return, and that he could be gone for a very long time.

The doctor eventually gave up trying to find him, which was a good thing since more than 40 years later Dayton was still using that right foot when he told this story. On occasion he did have to give special attention to his feet, and both continued to pain him over the years. He was sometimes forced to sleep in a chair at night and use tight hose because they hurt so badly, but the feet were still attached and working up to the end, in spite of a very determined Army doctor.

Amongst his personal papers is a form dated 26th January 1947 that refers to Dayton's feet being frostbitten during the Battle of the Bulge. It was recommended that Dayton be issued low quarter shoes and be allowed to wear them except on special occasions such as "command inspections, formal reviews and parades." This recommendation came from Captain R. G. Hamill, an army surgeon, shown on the next page.

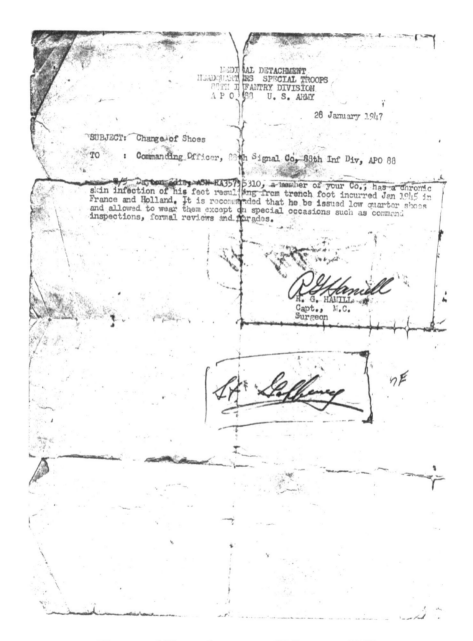

Change of Shoes document, 28 January 1947.

Marta

When the war in Europe came to an end, it appeared Dayton was destined for the Pacific. Then atomic bombs were dropped on Hiroshima and Nagasaki, and Japan was forced to surrender. This changed the Army's plan to ship Dayton to the Pacific.

All the tank destroyer battalions, including the 605th T.D. Battalion, were issued orders on the 20th June 1945 to begin deactivating, causing Dayton and other members of the 605th to be placed into other battalions. A few months later in the autumn of 1945, after first transferring to the 628th T.D. Battalion, Dayton received orders attaching him to the 740th Tank Battalion. With World War II over, he was stationed in Witzenhausen, Germany as a radio operator.

From a 740th Tank Battalion Association Newsletter, Mark Hatchel wrote "Witzenhausen is where radio operator PFC. Dayton Edie was sent to join the 740th Tank Battalion during the occupation of Germany. Witzenhausen, Germany was a gathering point for the Americans and British to round up as many German scientists and as much technology as possible to keep it from the Russians."[10] The future head of NASA, Wernher Von Braun, was one of the German scientists processed through Witzenhausen.

The time Dayton spent with the 740th was short, but it ended up being the favorite unit in which he served. He officially joined the 740th Tank Battalion Headquarters 17th September 1945 and worked as phone operator and messenger until 27th March 1946.

A young German girl about Dayton's age worked on a different floor in the same building in Witzenhausen. Her name was Marta Dietrich, and she worked as a translator for the Americans. Marta was known as Operator 12.

The Burgermeister of Limberg, Germany had personally asked her to be a switchboard operator for the Americans and she had accepted. Marta, at 19, found herself working for her former enemy.

---

[10] Hatchel, *The 740th Tank Battalion Association Newsletter*, 2.

Dayton was actually Marta's boss, which was probably the only time he held that position.

Growing up, Marta Dietrich had been called Marlee by her friends, so when she answered the switchboard she always said, "Marlee Dietrich speaking." With her name so similar to the famous German American actress Marlene Dietrich, the GIs teased Marta incessantly about being the beautiful actress. Marta said it took years for her to understand what the fuss was all about.

Marta was ideal for her position as she was fluent in numerous languages. She either spoke or understood five languages: German, English, French, Italian, and Dutch, and this was key to securing her phone operator/translator job. The other thing that helped Marta get the job was the fact she had a passport. That job eventually led to her meeting the man she would marry and spend the rest of her life with—Dayton Edie.

Marta had caught the eye of the slight but dashing Dayton. He asked her out on a date, and she accepted. The two dated for five years. Even when he was away, Dayton always wrote and stayed in touch with his Marta. He continued to send food and other supplies to Marta and her family and eventually to many others in her hometown of Diez.

Dayton's German girlfriend was born on the 21st February 1926 in the German town of Diez. Marta was named after her grandmother, Martha Erle, known as Leni. Marta's middle name of Liesel, German for Elisabeth, was given to her because it was the name of her mother's sister. This same aunt stood by her side on her wedding day.

Marta's father was Hermann Dietrich, born in July 1902. Hermann was from Altendiez, a village about three kilometers from Diez. In November 1905 Marta's mother was born in Diez, Germany, which is near Limburg, Germany. Her maiden name was Leni Erle. Hermann and Leni married in 1925, and almost a year later their only child Marta was born.

One month before she died, Marta's grandmother, Martha Erle wrote the following poem for her granddaughter Marta on 23rd February 1935:

> Profound peace in the troubles of the world
> Quiet strength that holds up under tribulations,
> A love that bends down toward misery,

And a humility that bows to God in reverence,
A joy, which like a bright sunlight beam
Breaks through even the darkest and fate laden clouds,
A strong unswerving courage,
Ready to dare just about anything,
A never tiring enduring patience
With your neighbor's weaknesses or fault,
And a faith that like an eagle's wings
Soars upward into the heavenly kingdom,
Finding nothing impossible nor too difficult,
This is my wish for you, ---
What more would you need?

For much of the war, Marta and her family had been uncertain exactly what had happened to her father, Hermann Dietrich. In civilian life he was an engineer who worked on railroads, so when war with Russia began in 1941 he followed the German armies east, helping build rail lines for supply. In 1944 when the tide of war turned, Hermann Dietrich was captured by the Russians. Most Germans captured by Russians never returned home with over 90% of them starved or worked to death by their Russian captors, if they were not killed outright.

In 1946 Marta had not heard from her father in more than two years, and everyone assumed he was dead. One day, when she was not at college, Marta and her mother started to hear a lot of noise. The noise was a celebration coming from the people of Diez gathered around Marta's Father. Ragged and shoeless, Hermann had walked from Russia back to Diez after being released by his captors. The Russians had kept him alive because he was mechanical and able to repair watches and other devices for them. He never knew the reason they decided to let him go, but he wasn't about to question it. So with no shoes on his feet, Marta's father walked home from Siberia in 1946.

Marta, at one time still had a "Hitler Youth" shirt from when she was a little girl. She explained that the Germans did not have the Boy or Girl Scouts, but instead they had the Path Finders. Many German boys and girls became Path Finders. Not long after Hitler's rise, the Path Finders and other similar German youth organizations all became Hitler Youth.

That meant all Path Finders were registered Nazis, whether they liked it or not. The Dietrich family owned a radio they pulled out during the war, waiting for the BBC to broadcast. It was against the law to listen to the BBC, but they did it anyway because it was the only dependable source of news. The family waited patiently by the radio until a bong sound came across the airwaves, followed by, "Hello, this is London calling."

Young Marta.

Young Dayton.

Marta and Dayton with Marta's father.

CARE

In 1945 when the American soldiers took over Diez, many of them immediately gave items like chocolate bars and chewing gum from their personal rations to the local residents. American soldiers throughout occupied Germany became friends with the German people, because they helped the hungry Germans get food and other necessities. Dayton and many other soldiers across occupied Germany did all they could to help the people in towns they occupied. These GI donations began what would become known as CARE. Officially started in 1946, CARE is an international organization and still exists today.

During occupation and after the war, the German people were starving and in dire need of food. When Marta received chewing gum for the first time she didn't know what it was and ate it. She swallowed piece after piece until she was told she wasn't supposed to eat it. Marta said she ate so much gum that it's probably still in her stomach now.

Dayton and other GIs continued giving rations to the locals even after the war was over. Some, like Dayton, continued to send care packages after they left. Eventually, CARE reached all the way back to the states, and many Americans sent food to relieve the suffering of the German people. When cornmeal first arrived from America, the Germans had no idea what it was and didn't know what to do with it. Cornmeal and gum were just two of the items the Germans had to learn about. Like my friend, World War II veteran and Silver Star recipient Harold G. Bradley said, "The United States did more for its defeated enemies than any other country in history."

When unable to visit Marta and her family, Dayton continued sending everything he could from his base in Trieste, Italy. Later, he also sent items to many of her neighbors, including the mayor. The mayor was the same man who had recommended Marta work as a phone operator for the Americans. Dayton was practically keeping the town supplied with food.

Marta said, "My mother fell in love with Dayton before I did." Many of the citizens of Diez were pretty fond of Dayton as well.

Decades later, Dayton and Marta were recognized by CARE, and the two of them even appeared in a commercial for the organization.

This is Marta's beautiful picture of the two of them together from the commercial shoot for CARE.

As much as Dayton should be remembered for his heroic actions, especially those at the Battle of the Bulge, my guess is he would be honored to be remembered as one of the founders and early supporters of CARE.

Dayton and Marta in a CARE photo.

Liberated by the Enemy

It was a fortunate thing to be occupied by the Americans, since no German wanted to be overrun by the Russians. German civilians who had the misfortune to fall under Russian control, often found themselves enslaved behind the Iron Curtain for decades. Germany became two separate countries of East and West, remaining that way until 1989.

In March of 1945 when Americans first marched into Diez to occupy the town, Marta said the locals felt liberated by their enemy. A curfew was put into place and in the beginning of the occupation, the German population of Diez could only be out between twelve noon and five o'clock.

At first, the Americans were under strict orders not to fraternize with the civilian population. As time went on and the rules over fraternizing relaxed, the Americans became friendly with the locals, offering them rations and other supplies. At one point U.S. soldiers even taught the German boys how to play baseball. In the beginning, when Diez was occupied by Americans everything got better. Unfortunately for the people of Diez, Allied Supreme Commander General Dwight D. Eisenhower changed the occupied zones and gave the French control over their section of Germany. By the time Dayton and Marta were working together and dating, the French had taken over control of her hometown.

When French soldiers first marched into town, the German boys expected the French to be as friendly as the Americans. After their defeat in 1940, the French had endured years of occupation by the Germans. The French had absolutely no affection for the Germans. When the German boys ran up to the French soldiers, the children were greeted by French boots and rifle butts. The French soldiers had no use for Germans, not even the little ones.

Even though the French were occupying Diez, Dayton still managed to see Marta on occasion. Dayton never did smoke. He always kept the cigarettes in his rations for trade. He used good old American tobacco to bribe the French so he could continue to visit his pretty German Fraulein. In most cases Dayton was friendly with the French soldiers he regularly encountered on his visits to Marta.

However, one particular evening ended rather badly. Dayton had gone to Marta's home and was visiting her inside. Outside the house, a drunken French soldier started yelling and staggering about, even occasionally firing off his rifle. The French soldier fired into the air first, and then his random fire began hitting the Dietrich house and other neighboring homes. This went on and on until Dayton had enough of it. Fearing somebody would be hit by a stray bullet, he went outside the house and confronted the Frenchman. Dayton held the French soldier in a ditch full of water until he passed. I've never been quite sure if 'passed' meant passed out, or passed until the French soldier was dead. Some things I'm better off not knowing.

Before the final defeat of Japan and end of World War II, Dayton secured a position as a security guard for President Truman at the Potsdam Conference. Marta has a blurry picture of Truman, but you can make out the white hat. The picture was taken by Dayton. President Truman did not want his guards to be seen, so Dayton and the other guards were all inside of buildings or out of sight. Dayton snapped a blurry picture of the President in the back of his car as it was driving by. Guarding generals and bridges during World War II had helped secure Dayton a position on President Truman's security detail at the Potsdam Conference.

The Potsdam Conference took place from 17th July to 2nd August 1945. Security for high value targets was a primary job for the CIC going back to the days of the Manhattan Project. The Manhattan Project was the codename for the Atomic Energy Program of the United States during World War II.

Regarding the Manhattan Project, "The part played by the CIC in keeping this awesome Project absolutely secret and secure was crucial."[11]

---

[11] Sayer and Botting, *America's Secret Army*, 71

Photo Dayton took of President Truman at the Potsdam Conference.

Skills of a Farmer Turned Soldier

Everyone seemed big to him, but Dayton always said the German soldiers they captured were giants. Generally, the German soldier was big with broad shoulders, and at the time Dayton was terribly envious. Toward the end of the war however, they mainly faced young German boys or old men.

The practice of using Hitler Jugend (Hitler Youth) in combat started in Normandy during the Invasion. The boys had been convinced by Hitler that Germany's fate rested on their small shoulders. The young German boys literally threw themselves at the American lines, attacking in an almost fanatical way. They charged right at the Americans, firing their weapons as they came! Dayton and other GIs hated to do it, but it was always kill or be killed.

However, before it came to the end, GIs typically fought against the big broad shouldered Germans during World War II. Dayton always wished he could be GI Joe big. He wanted to be broad like the Germans, even though he ended up surviving an amazing number of engagements, possibly thanks to his diminutive size.

When facing off against the big Germans Dayton always preferred the Garand rifle over the M1 carbine. He said when using the M1 carbine you could hit and kill a German soldier, but sometimes it just knocked them down. With the carbine's light stopping power a big wounded German might die eventually, but meanwhile he could sometimes lay waiting for an American to come closer, and then kill the American first! On the other hand if you hit a German soldier with the more powerful Garand rifle, he usually went down for the count leaving no worry he'd get up and come after you later.

During the Korean War when he was fighting against the Chinese and North Koreans, Dayton said he preferred the M1 carbine over the Garand for two reasons. First, any time the North Koreans or Chinese attacked, they always came in waves, sending one wave after another at the American lines. The M1 carbine had a 30 round magazine; much better than the eight shots of the Garand rifle.

With so many of the enemy coming toward you at once, having 22 more rounds in each clip was certainly advantageous!

The second reason he preferred the M1 carbine in Korea was the stature of the enemy. North Koreans and Chinese tended to be much smaller than the broad shouldered German soldiers. Because of their more diminutive size, when a North Korean or Chinese was hit by the smaller round of the M1 carbine, they usually went down for the count. There were occasional exceptions to this rule, and the thick cotton uniforms of the Chinese slowed down the rounds from the M1 carbine. But generally the M1 carbine with its 30 round magazine was better at taking down large groups of enemy soldiers.

Over his military career, Dayton fired thousands and thousands of rounds. Quite a few of those rounds were from the .50 caliber machine gun. The .50 caliber machine gun was Dayton's favorite weapon. He often said, "With the .50 caliber, if you could see it, you could hit it." Sadly, firing off all those rounds resulted in permanent hearing loss, which required Dayton to use a hearing aid later in life.

The length of time a machine gun position could rapid fire was around three minutes, but the average life span of an active machine gunner was only two and a half minutes. If a machine gun position continued non-stop firing, enemy mortars soon opened up on it. Of course this revealed where the enemy mortar crews were located, but they would risk it to get one of our machine gun positions. The mortar crews typically had a company of German infantry alongside them for protection.

A .50 usually brought mortar and artillery response, a .30 usually didn't, so soldiers like .50s around, but not too close. What a machine gunner needed to do was shoot off a short burst. Even better than a short burst of fire was to try and squeeze off just a few single rounds at a time. Believing it to be the best way to handle a machine gun, Dayton always preferred squeezing off single rounds.

Another rule of thumb, Dayton said was never to fire on a straight line too long. The enemy could easily follow a straight line back to the weapon laying down that fire. To help keep their position from being located by the enemy, many soldiers would remove the tracer rounds if any were in the ammo belt. There was a fine line between how long you fired and making sure you sprayed that fire. Being a machine gunner was a very dangerous job.

More on the .50 and in order to better explain how powerful this weapon was on the battlefield, "...originally developed as an aircraft weapon the Browning M2 was brought into use with ground troops as a possible anti-tank gun and later as a general heavy support weapon. It has been widely used in the anti-aircraft role, and is still to be found in service with armies all over the world. Weight: 84 lb. Rate of fire: 500 rpm. Muzzle velocity: 2950 fps."[12]

---

[12] Ian V. Hogg, *The Complete Machine Gun* (New York: Exeter Books, in association with Phoebus, 1979), 52.

Road Trips to Yugoslavia

After World War II was over and before 1950, Dayton was sent on at least two missions into Yugoslavia. This happened when he was operating out of Trieste, Italy. He never gave an exact year when these missions took place, only saying they happened after the start of the Cold War.

During this time Dayton's rank rose from temporary to permanent technician 5th grade on the 17th May 1946. His next promotion was to corporal on the 31st July 1948, and then to sergeant on the 9th June 1949. He served with the 18th Signal Service Company.

The West feared that any Russian attack would include an armored thrust tearing through the Balkans. There was little knowledge of the few accessible roads, especially in Yugoslavia, and if the Russians attacked through that area western nations wanted knowledge of the roads and surrounding terrain.

Dayton was sent into Yugoslavia twice to map out roads and study the terrain. On both missions he was out of uniform, wearing clothing that helped him blend in with the locals. To hear Dayton tell it, these operations were very much like "Mission Impossible." Had he been caught, he would have been disavowed and left on his own.

He told me about those two operations during the 1990's when the United States had gotten involved in the ethnic fighting and atrocities resulting from the breakup of Yugoslavia. It was Dayton's strong opinion we had no business meddling there thinking we could stop the violence. Dayton knew we could only stop the feuding for a while as long as military forces were positioned there, but the minute we left, the feuds would continue. "In that region there were blood feuds and vows of revenge that went back centuries."

On two of his missions into Yugoslavia, Dayton witnessed Yugoslavian soldiers being relieved of guard duty. On both occasions, he watched from his hiding place as a Yugoslavian sentry, after having been relieved, turned his back to the soldier who had relieved him. Not once, but on two separate occasions, Dayton watched as the soldier there to relieve his comrade turned and brought an axe down in the middle of the first soldier's back! After witnessing this treatment two different times, he decided these people had serious issues with each other.

On another mission where he was undercover and out of uniform, money was sewn into the lining of his clothing in case it was needed. He slept during the day while doing the work related to his mission at night, which was the job of mapping roads.

One night when he was out surveying, he decided to sneak into a fig grove to grab a few figs. After sneaking into the grove, he climbed up a nearby tree to pick the best fruits near the top. On his way back down, a woman came along catching him by surprise. When she saw him, the woman was obviously scared, and she started making an awful ruckus. Quickly ripping into one of the hidden pockets in his clothes, Dayton pulled out the money and handed it to the woman.

Whether from shock or satisfaction, complete silence replaced the noise she'd been making. With a smile, the woman took the money and went about her business. Dayton didn't mind losing the money. He was just happy she'd stopped making noise that could have gotten him shot.

Later, Dayton figured the woman had made so much noise because she was doing the same thing he was doing; stealing figs! After seeing him, the woman must have thought she'd been caught. The only difference was she ended up getting paid for her night's work.

Dayton and others worked out of Trieste from 1946-1949, infiltrating communist controlled areas in Eastern Europe including Yugoslavia.

Dayton (left) with a fellow soldier
while he was stationed in Trieste, Italy.

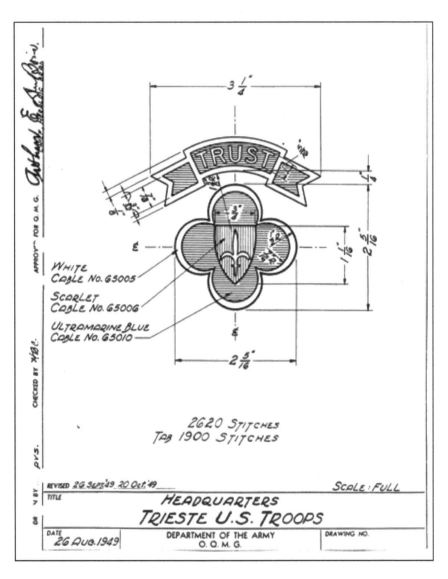

Trieste United States Troops (TRUST) shoulder sleeve insignia.

Trieste United States Troops (TRUST) shoulder sleeve insignia.

One Edie Becomes Three

On the 1st of May 1950, Marta Dietrich married Dayton Edie, and together they became Dayton and Marta Edie. The couple married at the Cathedral Tower in Frankfurt, Germany. The construction of the great cathedral started in 1413.

In 1950 however, the church was not yet repaired from damage done by bombs during World War II. The Cathedral Tower in Frankfurt was not used for services after the war. Instead its primary task was hosting weddings.

The town of Frankfurt had been targeted so much during the war that by 1950 ceiling and wall sections were still missing from the church. The missing sections allowed sunlight to spill into the church during the Edie's ceremony. The beaming sunshine made everything seem majestic and beautiful while exposing the devastation of the war.

It was not easy for the two young people to marry. There are multiple forms indicating everything required in order for a marriage between an American soldier and a German civilian to take place. For example, one document was an Affidavit of Support that Dayton had to fill out showing he could support his young wife. He had to present proof of his worth/value in savings, soldier's deposit, cash on hand ($700), U. S. govt. bonds, etc.

The U.S. government required Marta's birth certificate and a form clearing her of venereal diseases. Another document pertaining to her involvement in the Hitler Youth indicates she had been de-Nazified. Marta's classification as a Nazi had come like so many other German children's from her involvement with the Pathfinders.

In order for her to enter the United States after their marriage, she had to be de-Nazified in accordance with Control Directives 24 and 38 under the category of Youth Amnesty. Marta also filled out a Petition for Issuance of Immigration Visa.

Dayton lost his Top Secret clearance levels because of his marriage to Marta. His Sergeant at the time pleaded with him not to marry. The Sergeant said Dayton was not only nuts for marrying because it would cost him his clearance, but he also said a German woman would drive him crazy as he got older! On one service record dated 28th April 1950, it states "Not eligible for assignment to EUCOM by reason of marriage to German National."

Dayton didn't care. He married her anyway.

Not only did Marta complete the Petition for Issuance of Immigration Visa for the United States of America, but she also needed a release from officials in Germany. Numerous forms were required for them to marry. On one document, a Letter of Acquiescence Dayton had to answer the question why he wanted to marry. He wrote, "Because I love her." On her section of the document, Marta wrote, "Because I love him."

With all the forms properly filled out, Dayton and Marta were granted permission to marry.

The newly wedded couple then traveled to the United States, arriving first in New York. From there they traveled to Carntown, Kentucky where Dayton had grown up. One marriage document dated 1st June 1950, indicates Dayton was allowed 30 days leave to visit RT 1 Box 89, Pendleton, Kentucky.

In Dayton's hometown, most of the residents seemed to know all about his heroics at the Battle of the Bulge, probably thanks to the many 605th Tank Destroyer Battalion members who were residents of eastern Kentucky. When they arrived, the people in the town treated Dayton like a hero. The townspeople wanted the couple to stay there and live in Carntown, even offering them land and a house. Marta had no idea what Dayton had done during the war, so she didn't understand why everyone seemed so impressed.

Dayton told his bride they could not stay in Carntown, because too many people there would ask him questions. He didn't tell her, but he was uncomfortable being asked about the Battle of the Bulge and his covert missions. He was not ready to discuss his military experiences.

The happy couple left Kentucky, but Dayton was still active in the U.S. Army. They traveled to California.

Michael Clarence Edie was born on the 4th February 1951 in San Francisco, CA. There were three Edies now, and they lived in an apartment in the Richmond area. For most of his time in California, Dayton was stationed at Ft. Mason.

In the early 1950s Marta found herself in California, far from Germany and alone most of the time with little Michael. While living at the apartment in Richmond, Marta decided to go to the campus at University of California Berkley to see what she had to do to take a few English classes. Since Marta lived in the United States, she wanted to improve her English. For Germans and Austrians it has always been incredibly important to speak perfect English.

All Marta wanted was to study basic English, but she had to take an entrance exam to enroll in any of the classes the university offered. She took the exam and waited for the results. She scored a 98% on the entrance exam, so the university not only let her enroll in English, but because of her high score, the university had her skip basic English and enrolled Marta in upper level classes.

In one upper such course she collided with her professor. They were reading William Shakespeare, and the professor stopped Marta in midsentence. The professor told Marta that in all his years of teaching he had always wanted more emotion from his students when they were reading. However, she was the first student from whom he ever wanted less from.

WIR HABEN GEHEIRATET

Dayton Edie

Marta Liesel Edie
geb. DIETRICH

Butler/Ky. U. S. A.   Diez/Lahn
                                                     Altstadtstraße 31
1. Mai 1950

Die kirchliche Trauung findet in der Nicolaikirche in Frankfurt statt.

The Edies wedding invitation in German.

```
WITH THE UNITED STATES ARMY      )
                                 ) SS    AFFIDAVIT OF SUPPORT
AT FRANKFURT-AM-MAIN, GERMANY    )
```

I, Dayton Edie Sgt RA 357 953 10, being duly sworn, depose and say:

1. I am a citizen of the United States of America; was born at Cincinnati Ohio on 9 February 1925, and reside at Route 1, Box 89 at Butler Kentucky.

2. The names and ages and relationships to me of persons already dependent on me for support are:

   Clarence Edie   age 70   father

3. The names and ages of the prospective immigrants are:

   Martha Liesal Dietrich   age 24   bride

4. I am financially able to undertake the obligation of giving full support to dependents listed above, and have the following assets:

   a. Bank accounts with total of $300:00 deposited
   b. Soldier's deposits in the amount of $800:00
   c. Cash on hand in the amount of $700:00
   d. US Gov't War Bonds in the amount of $303:78
   e. Securities, bonds, or stocks presently worth $ none
   f. Real estate valued at $ none
   g. Automobile valued at $ none
   h. Present annual income $2160:00
   i. Insurance in the amount of $10,000:00

5. The following named persons are my relatives and are ready, willing and able to help me in case of an emergency during which I might have need for additional funds:

   Edward H. Turner   Grace Baker

                               Dayton Edie
                               Sgt Dayton Edie
                               RA 357 953 10

On this 21 day of April 1950, before me, the undersigned officer, personally appeared Sgt Dayton Edie and after being duly sworn did subscribe his name to the within instrument and acknowledged to me that he did execute the same freely and voluntarily for the purposes therein contained and that the facts recited are true.

                               Vaughn H Banks
                               VAUGHN H BANKS
                               1st Lt   Inf
                               Summary Court Officer

Affidavit of Support in order to marry Marta, 21 April 1950.

THE UNITED STATES OF AMERICA
VETERANS' ADMINISTRATION
WASHINGTON, D. C.

National Service Life Insurance

DATE INSURANCE EFFECTIVE ___MARCH 18, 1943___

CERTIFICATE No. N- __5 380 605__

This Certifies That ___DAYTON EDIE___ has applied for insurance in the amount of $ __10,000.__ , payable in case of death.

Subject to the payment of the premiums required, this insurance is granted under the authority of The National Service Life Insurance Act of 1940, and subject in all respects to the provisions of such Act, of any amendments thereto, and of all regulations thereunder, now in force or hereafter adopted, all of which, together with the application for this insurance, and the terms and conditions published under authority of the Act, shall constitute the contract.

Administrator of Veterans' Affairs.

Countersigned at Washington, D. C.

April 3, 1943
(Date)

M. Venezia
Registrar.

Mr. Clarence Wait Edie
R.R. #1
Butler, Kentucky

Insurance Form 360

1943 document.

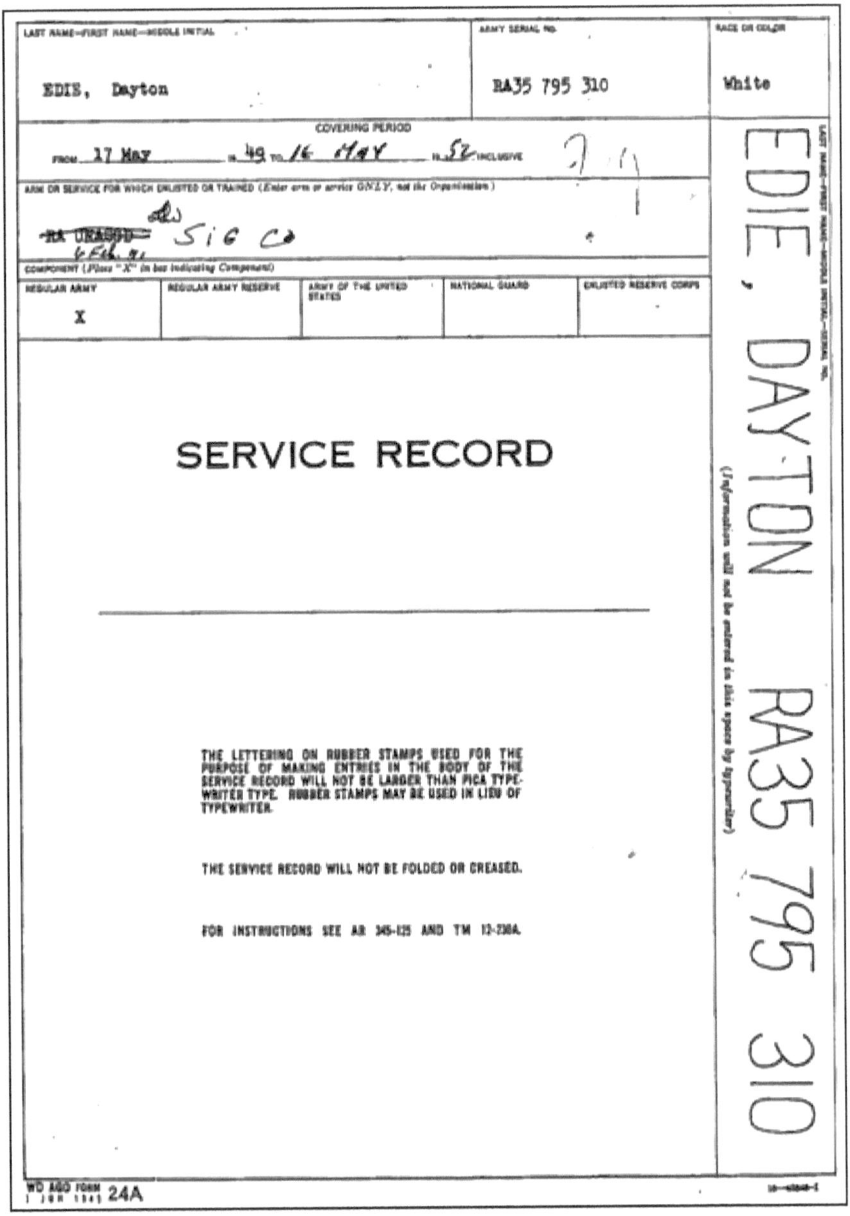

LAST NAME—FIRST NAME—MIDDLE INITIAL

EDIE, Dayton

ARMY SERIAL NO.

RA35 795 310

RACE OR COLOR

White

COVERING PERIOD

FROM 17 May 19 49 TO 16 MAY 19 52 INCLUSIVE

ARM OR SERVICE FOR WHICH ENLISTED OR TRAINED (Enter arm or service ONLY, not the Organization)

~~RA UNASGD~~ Sig Co

COMPONENT (Place "X" in box indicating Component)

REGULAR ARMY	REGULAR ARMY RESERVE	ARMY OF THE UNITED STATES	NATIONAL GUARD	ENLISTED RESERVE CORPS
X				

SERVICE RECORD

THE LETTERING ON RUBBER STAMPS USED FOR THE PURPOSE OF MAKING ENTRIES IN THE BODY OF THE SERVICE RECORD WILL NOT BE LARGER THAN PICA TYPEWRITER TYPE. RUBBER STAMPS MAY BE USED IN LIEU OF TYPEWRITER.

THE SERVICE RECORD WILL NOT BE FOLDED OR CREASED.

FOR INSTRUCTIONS SEE AR 345-125 AND TM 12-230A.

LAST NAME—FIRST NAME—MIDDLE INITIAL—SERIAL NO.

EDIE, DAYTON RA35 795 310

(Information will not be entered in this space by typewriter)

WD AGO FORM 24A

Document stating Dayton not eligible for EUCOM.

SECTION 9—REMARKS—ADMINISTRATIVE	
DATE	REMARK

17 May 49- Discharged 16 May 49 per AR 615-360 ETS Enl 17 May 49 for RA Unasgd (Own Vacancy) per Cir 66 DA 48.
17 May 49- 36 mos continuous sv toward GCM
17 May 49- LAC completed 19 Oct 48- Report filed Hq TRUST APO 209
17 May 49- PBI (Cryptographic) completed 1 Mar 49 Report Filed G-2, Hq TRUST APO 209, US Army
19 Oct 49. Overseas tour extended from 21 Oct 49 to 21 Jun 19 per 4th Ind Hq Frankfurt Mil Post APO 757 dtd 17 Oct 49. 2YAPR50 NOT ELIGIBLE FOR ASSIGNMENT TO EUCOM BY REASON OF MARRIAGE TO A GERMAN NATIONAL AUTH 600-1751 LTR 21 JUN 49 DEARSE EM MARRIED MARTA LIESEL DIETRICH AT FRANKFURT/MAIN GERMANY 2 APR 50
9 Aug 50- Compl 7 yrs sv 1 April 50
25 Aug 50- Auth Sep Rats eff 24 Aug 50 per Par 7 SO 165 Hq OAB, Oakland 14, Calif. dtd 24 Aug 50
29 Jan 51- Auth Sep Rats eff 26 Jan 51 per Par 6 SO 19 Hq OAB, Oakland 14, California. dtd 26 Jan 51
6 Feb 51- Clarence M. Ellis born to EM 4 Feb 51.
3 Apr 51- Compl 8 yrs sv 1 Apr 51.
24 Jul 51- Three (3) year enlistment of 17 May 49 extended for one (1) year under the provisions of the Act of 19 Jun 51 (Public Law 51 82 Congress.
19 Dec 51- OJT Training completed 26 Oct 49
DD Form 2A 20 094 165 issued 7 Feb 51.
One year involuntary extension of enlistment reduced to 10 months per DA MSG 902642 dtd 6 Mar 52
COMPLETED 31 MONTHS 10 DAYS S.C. TOWARDS G.C.M. CLASP.

Document stating Dayton not eligible for EUCOM.

Dayton with Michael at his side

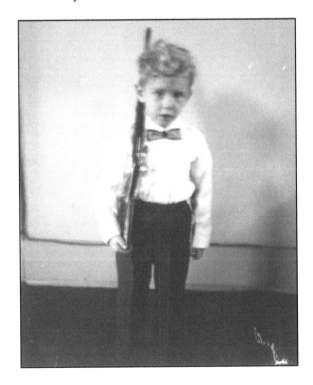

Michael.

Dayton with Michael.

Watching an A-bomb Explode

While Marta took courses at University of California Berkley to perfect her English, Dayton was in California training men for combat in Korea. During this time, he received orders to report immediately to Nevada. Dayton was flown by small plane to the Nevada Desert, where he ended up witnessing an atomic explosion.

The test of this atom bomb took place on the 1st of May 1952. The name of the location for the test site was Desert Rock. Dayton's clearance levels were reinstated. He was ordered to the test site after being personally requested by someone, but he wasn't sure just who. His exact orders were to fix up communications, but when he arrived at the site, a Marine sergeant had already completed more than two thirds of the wiring. With the Marine sergeant there, Dayton knew he wasn't really needed, but he knew if he left early he'd be in trouble later.

When the atom bomb was detonated, Dayton was in a concrete bunker located approximately a mile away. He and several other men observed the explosion through a thick glass window from inside the bunker. All the other men in the bunker were officers. He and the officers were at a safe distance, but that was not the case for several U.S. Marines. Those poor Marines were given orders to march toward the blast during the test. They marched as close as possible right up to the blast, until they were no longer able to withstand the heat and were forced to turn back. They were being used as test subjects by the army to see how close soldiers could get to an atomic explosion before having to turn away. Dayton believed every one of those poor Marines perished from cancer or other diseases related to the fallout from that blast.

In the protected bunker, Dayton recognized one of the officers, a guy named Lavelle whom he had met once before. Dayton didn't say anything to Lavelle, and years later he told me he was glad he hadn't. If he had spoken to or been seen by Lavelle, Dayton believed the officer would have ordered him to report to his office and would have then requested he be transferred to the chemical branch of the army. He was not sure, but he believed it was Lavelle who had requested he attend the explosion.

Dayton had no desire to join the chemical branch of the army. Everyone who witnessed the atomic explosion was given a certificate to prove they had seen it. Sgt. Dayton Edie was then taken to a bus station where he rode a Greyhound back to his base in California. At the bus station, he tore the certificate into tiny pieces, disposing of it properly.

There are four "Certificate of Training" diplomas in Dayton's personal papers from the 1950s.

Phase III Atomic Energy Indoctrination Course, 12-13 July 1950.

Training in Military Justice Matters 20 August 1951.

Chemical, Biological and Radiological Defense, 26 October 1951.

Instruction in the Geneva Convention of 1949, 13-19 November 1951.

Psychic Sergeant

From the Nevada test site, Dayton returned to his duties readying soldiers for deployment to Korea. Not long after, he received orders for deployment to Korea. Dayton left San Francisco on the 12th October 1952, traveling to Yokohama, Japan. He arrived there on the 23rd October, and stayed in Japan for four days. From there he was at sea for three days, until landing at Inchon, Korea on the 30th October.

Officially from 10th October 1952 until 27th July 1953, Sgt. Dayton Edie served in Korea as the Communications Chief - Communications Platoon, HQ CO, 179th Infantry Regiment 45th Infantry Division. Dayton would fight against both Chinese and North Korean soldiers.

By the time fighting in Korea came to an uneasy ceasefire at the end of July 1953, Dayton's squad had started referring to him as their Psychic Sergeant. Dayton had precisely predicted two separate attacks by the enemy with no tangible evidence to support his predictions. This convinced the men in his platoon he was psychic.

The first psychic event came when Dayton and the other men found themselves manning a defensive position in Korea. It had rained all night and into the morning. After a rain, cotton emits a strong, distinctive odor, and once you get a whiff of that smell, you'll never forget it. Right before the attack Dayton smelled the scent of wet cotton. He knew Chinese soldiers wore a two piece cotton uniform, and he had a pretty good idea of what was about to happen. He told the men to prepare and spread the word. They were going to be attacked by the Chinese.

The men did as ordered, but since no one else had heard of an impending attack, they all thought it was a drill. That theory came crashing down when waves of Chinese showed up trying to overrun American lines. Suddenly, hundreds upon hundreds of Chinese were charging straight at U.S. defenses.

They came too fast for Dayton to say, "I told you so."

The first wave of Chinese soldiers charged the American lines only to be cut down, as were the following waves. The assault was tense, but the Americans held strong, repelling everything the Chinese threw at them. The Americans were victorious having survived the Chinese attack.

When the smoke cleared, the 179th Infantry Regiment eventually moved from that area of Korea. Now when Dayton gave orders, the soldiers jumped. They couldn't figure out how their sergeant had correctly predicted the Chinese attack. It was more than a little spooky. But the result was they no longer doubted him when he made a prediction.

Six months after the attack by the Chinese in early July of 1953, Dayton and his men were in an area where only North Koreans would oppose them.

Based on updates from headquarters, he knew with absolute certainty no Chinese soldiers were in their immediate vicinity near Mundung-Ni, Korea, which is north of the 38th Parallel. Once again there was no reason to suspect an attack. Dayton and his men were dug in, forming a defensive line atop a ridge.

Dayton's father had an old saying learned from years of working in the coal mines. "Whatever direction the critters are headed, you head in that same direction!" His father had taught Dayton animals could sense disaster before humans ever see it coming. That piece of wisdom came to him in Korea as he stood atop that windy ridge.

Dayton began seeing small animals coming out of the foliage and undergrowth in front of his men all along their defensive line, heading directly at them. The animals, mostly small rodents, were coming straight for their positions as if something was driving them forward. No one else seemed to pay much attention to scared creatures, but Dayton remembered what his father had told him and sensed danger was imminent. With no explanation, he yelled to his men that the North Koreans were coming. Prepare for an attack!

His men wasted no time. As predicted, within minutes North Koreans were charging at the American defenses.

Just like in the battle with the Chinese six months earlier, the American Soldiers had no idea how Dayton had known of an oncoming attack by North Koreans. It perplexed them even more that he always seemed to know which of their enemies they were about to face.

When they attacked, the North Koreans and Chinese both sent waves of soldiers, to break through American lines. With North Korean attacks, their first wave usually consisted of the weak, wounded, and older members of their unit. These first waves were not usually armed with the best weapons. Many times they carried only machetes, knives, sticks, spears, and poles. Even though those first waves did not carry modern firearms, Dayton said, "Hundreds upon hundreds of machetes coming at you was as scary as any firearm you ever saw."

If necessary to motivate them into charging at the Americans, the men in the first waves were liquored and doped up. The North Korean goal was to force the Americans to use up ammo on the old, weak, and sick. Then in the final wave of attacks, their most elite and best equipped soldiers charged the Americans. With their best troops attacking last, the North Koreans hoped the Americans would be low on ammo, worn down, or too exhausted to defend themselves.

Just as Dayton had predicted, wave after wave of North Koreans came charging straight at the American lines! Dayton gave orders to make every shot count and to use their ammo wisely. Right after the first waves attacked, an old North Korean soldier managed to get behind the American lines. Dayton happened to look back in time to see a doped up old man coming at him with a long sharpened pole. Barely able to move in time, he avoided a vital shot, but the old soldier still managed to stick the long pole into the bottom part of Dayton's calf.

By this time there was a much bigger threat than the pole sticking out of Dayton's leg. North Korean soldiers with modern weapons were headed for the American lines directly in front of his position. Dayton held the pole with one hand to keep the old North Korean from pulling it out and puncturing him again. With his other hand, he fired his pistol at the better armed enemy just in front of him. By saving his ammo for the better equipped North Koreans instead of using it on the crazy old man at the other end of the pole, Dayton managed to survive the battle. When asked about the crazy old man, due to a matter of necessity he said, "I eventually got around to taking care of that problem."

Twice, Dayton had predicted who was going to attack and when. None of Dayton's men figured out how he did it, so they started calling him the Psychic Sergeant. Dayton never let them in on the secret.

During his tour of duty in Korea, Dayton served with Dan Blocker. Blocker was later best known as Hoss Cartwright in the television series "Bonanza."

At the time, Blocker was not as big as he was in the show, but apparently he was mean as a snake. Blocker always carried a long lead pipe and vowed that if he ran out of ammo, he'd take as many enemy soldiers as he could down with that pipe. When Dayton ran into Blocker years later at reunions, the actor said he had raised his children as Swiss citizens so they would never have to fight in a war.

The 179th Infantry Regiment, 45th Infantry Division that both Dayton and Dan Blocker served in was awarded the Republic of Korea Presidential Unit Citation for actions from 10th December 1951 to 31st July 1953. The citation states, "During the Communist summer offensive of 1953, the 45th United States Infantry Division once again exhibited its fighting spirit and singleness of purpose as it frustrated enemy attacks and preserved vital positions on Sand Bag Castle, Heartbreak Ridge, and Christmas Hill."

Fighting in Korea ended on the 31st of July 1953.

A document dated 31st July 1953 is the form for the "Award of the Purple Heart." It states Sgt. Edie was wounded in the vicinity of Mundung-ni, Korea on the 11th July 1953 and is signed by Captain G.R.W. Warren. This document references the injury he received to his leg.

For Meritorious achievement in Ground Operations against the enemy (Korea, 10 October 1952 to 27 July 1953), Sgt. Dayton Edie was awarded the Bronze Star Medal.

One document asked, "What did the individual do that merits the award?" with the following explanation given: "M/Sgt. Edie organized his platoon in such a manner as to insure constant harmony, cooperation, and maximum efficiency under a combat situation! His platoon continually furnished the regimental headquarters with constant and efficient communications whether in a station or mobile situation." That document was dated 15th August 1953 and is signed by 1st Lt. Ralph McGill, Infantry Communications Platoon Leader.

Before leaving Korea, Dayton encountered an old North Korean woman who infuriated him. If she had been a man he would have popped her in the mouth. The old woman told Dayton that all great empires in the past had fallen and that someday America would fall as well. This may not seem like a big deal to people today. Back in the 1950's, America was on top of the world, and an old North Korean woman smarting off about the United States to a veteran like Dayton Edie did not go over well. He used to say at the time, it felt like the United States was invincible.

On the 8th August Dayton left from Pusan, Korea and arrived back in the United States at the Port of San Francisco on the 24th August 1953.

```
                    HEADQUARTERS 179TH INFANTRY
                              APO 86

GENERAL ORDERS                                        31 July 1953
NUMBER      30

                             Section I

                     AWARD OF THE PURPLE HEART

    Under the provisions of AR 600-45, a Purple Heart for wounds received in
action against the enemy at the places and on the dates indicated is awarded to:

→   Master Sergeant DAYTON EDIE, RA35795310, Infantry, United States Army,
Headquarters Company, 179th Infantry Regiment, wounded in action on 11 July 1953
in the vicinity of Kundung-ni, Korea. Entered the Federal service from California.

    Corporal NORMAN O LEDGETT, US56088661, Infantry, United States Army, Company
M, 179th Infantry Regiment, wounded in action on 10 June 1953 in the vicinity of
Paeam, Korea. State of entry into Federal service unknown.

    Private First Class DOMINGO CASTRO-LOPEZ, US50117861, Infantry, United States
Army, Headquarters Company, 179th Infantry Regiment, wounded in action on 20 July
1953 in the vicinity of Taegok, Korea. Entered the Federal service from Puerto
Rico.

                             Section II

              AWARD OF THE PURPLE HEART (OAK-LEAF CLUSTER)

    Under the provisions of AR 600-45, a Purple Heart (First Bronze Oak-Leaf
Cluster) for wounds received in action against the enemy at the place and on the
date indicated is awarded to:

    Master Sergeant EARL E HANEY RA10734654, Infantry, United States Army,
Company I, 179th Infantry Regiment, wounded in action on 18 June 1953 in the
vicinity of Sat'ae-ri, Korea. Entered the Federal service from Virginia.

                            Section III

                      REVOCATION OF GENERAL ORDERS

    So much of Section II (Award of the Purple Heart(Oak-Leaf Cluster)), General
Orders 28, this headquarters, 1953, pertaining to Master Sergeant J C RICHARDS JR,
RA38461246, Infantry, United States Army, Company K, 179th Infantry Regiment, is
revoked.

    So much of Section I (Award of the Purple Heart), General Orders 26, this
headquarters, 1953, pertaining to Master Sergeant EARL E HANEY, RA10734654,
Infantry, United States Army, Company I, 179th Infantry Regiment, is revoked.
```

Award of the Purple Heart.

```
                    HEADQUARTERS 179TH INFANTRY
                              APO 86

SPECIAL ORDERS                                    27 April 1953
NUMBER      102

    1. UP of AR 600-70, the following named enlisted men, Hq Co 179 Inf, are
hereby awarded the Combat Infantryman Badge for having satisfactorily performed
duties while assigned to an infantry unit engaged in active ground combat against
the enemy.

GRADE       NAME                          SN

PFC         LEMUEL D BURNS JR             RA13437929
PFC         DAVID L CONBOY                US51142919
SFC         DAYTON EDIE                   RA35795310
PFC         STANLEY L FISH                NG20376918
PFC         ALFRED F LEE                  US56135239
PFC         ROBERT E MORFORD              NG26143026
CPL         LOUIS SANTORO                 RA12390587
PVT-2       RICHARD J SIMON               US51428603
CPL         ROBERT P SWEENEY              US56114408
PFC         JAMES J YACCARINI             US55241999

    2. UP of AR 600-70, PFC EDUARDO SANCHEZ US56134163 Svc Co 179 Inf is hereby
awarded the Combat Infantryman Badge for having satisfactorily performed duties
while assigned to an infantry unit engaged in active ground combat against the
enemy.

    3. UP of AR 600-70, the following named officers and enlisted men, Co B 179
Inf are hereby awarded the Combat Infantryman Badge for having satisfactorily per-
formed duties while assigned to an infantry unit engaged in active ground combat
against the enemy.

GRADE       NAME                          SN

2D LT       ALEXANDER M CAPPELLI          0998772
2D LT       DONALD W NICOL                02102888
2D LT       PAUL T PESHKOFF               01877549
PVT-2       VICOMEDES L CELESTE           US50004189
PFC         ANDRES CLAUDIO-BERRIOS        US29207044
PVT-2       PERFECTO GONZALES-LEBRON      US50117175
PFC         GARLAND A HANCOCK JR          RA18389920
PFC         JOHN KOSTULAS                 RA12362745
PVT-2       JAMES H PLUMLEY               US52474395
PFC         HUBERT L WOOD                 RA19415905

    4. VOCO 19 Apr 53 transferring PFC ANDREW J HEMMEPLIGHT US53094309 from Co M
179 Inf to Hq Co 3 Bn 179 Inf EDCSA 19 Apr 53, is hereby confirmed and made of re-
cord, such order having been issued under exigencies which prevented issuance of
written order in advance.

    5. VOCO 22 Apr 53 transferring PFC THOMAS R DECKER US56145174 from Co I 179
Inf to Hq Co 3 Bn 179 Inf EDCSA 22 Apr 53, is hereby confirmed and made of record,
such order having been issued under exigencies which prevented issuance of written
order in advance.
```

Award of the Combat Infantry Badge.

```
                    HEADQUARTERS 45TH INFANTRY DIVISION
                                APO 86

GENERAL ORDERS                                         12 November 1953
NUMBER    621
                    AWARD OF THE BRONZE STAR MEDAL

     By direction of the President, under the provisions of Executive Order 9419,
4 February 1944 (Sec II, WD Bul 3, 1944), and pursuant to authority in AR 600-45,
the Bronze Star Medal for meritorious service in Korea in connection with military
operations against an armed enemy during the periods indicated is awarded to the
following named members of the United States Army:

     First Lieutenant JAMES H BECKWITH, JR, O1925875, Infantry, 19 May 1953 to
27 July 1953. Entered the Federal service from Georgia.

     First Lieutenant ROBERT D BOONE, O1933869, Medical Corps, 11 April 1953 to
27 July 1953. Entered the Federal service from Indiana.

     Second Lieutenant JACK R DEHM, O1931696, Artillery, 1 May 1953 to 27 July
1953. Entered the Federal service from Texas.

     Master Sergeant DAYTON EDIE, RA35795310, Infantry, 10 October 1952 to
27 July 1953. Entered the Federal service from Kentucky.

     Master Sergeant JOHN H MAINS, RA6713880, Artillery, 20 May 1953 to 27 July
1953. Entered the Federal service from New York.

     Sergeant First Class WILBUR H BELL, US56124513, Infantry, 18 June 1953 to
27 July 1953. Entered the Federal service from Idaho.

     Sergeant First Class WAYNE S KEEN, RA13394842, Infantry, 1 February 1953 to
27 July 1953. Entered the Federal service from Pennsylvania.

     Sergeant First Class JAMES O KELLY, RA26361947, Artillery, 14 January 1953
to 27 July 1953. Entered the Federal service from Iowa.

     Sergeant First Class EWELL O WINSLOW, US5524977, 8 August 1952 to
27 July 1953. Entered the Federal service from Indiana.

     Sergeant First Class EDWARD R LITTLE, RA6565606, Infantry, 27 September 1952
to 27 July 1953. State of entry into Federal service unknown.

     Sergeant First Class EARL B RAUSCH, JR, US55218560, Infantry, 15 January
1953 to 27 July 1953. State of entry into Federal service unknown.

     Sergeant First Class THOMAS J ROBERTS, RA35409772, Infantry, 8 January 1953
to 27 July 1953. Entered the Federal service from Ohio.

     Sergeant First Class ALFRED J SANDERS, US55221026, Infantry, 27 September
1952 to 27 July 1953. Entered the Federal service from Kansas.

     Sergeant First Class CLARENCE J SANDERS, US55142616, Infantry, 21 July 1952
to 31 May 1953. Entered the Federal service from North Dakota.

     Sergeant CLEVELAND BLACK, US53135710, Armor, 19 June 1953 to 27 July 1953.
Entered the Federal service from Alabama.
```

Award of the Bronze Star.

Dayton receiving the Bronze Star from Lt. Col. Willis E. Kooken, Battalion Commander, at Ft. Bragg, February 5, 1954.

Back to the States

In 1955 the Edies purchased a house near Dixie Highway not far from Ft. Knox, Kentucky. They bought one of the first three houses on the outskirts of Louisville. Shortly after buying their house, Dayton's son Michael came running up to him all excited. Michael was delighted because he had found an alligator. Little Michael was only five years old. He told Dayton he'd found an alligator in the ditch down by the railroad tracks and needed help catching it. Dayton assumed his son had seen a large lizard of some kind. He walked down to the tracks to see exactly what Michael had found, never expecting to see an actual alligator. After all they were in Louisville, Kentucky, not sunny Florida! Alligators are not indigenous to Kentucky since winter temperatures regularly drop below freezing.

Sure enough though, Michael was right! It was an alligator!

Someone had dumped the young reptile leaving it by the tracks. It was about a foot or two long. Dayton and Michael caught the alligator and took it home, keeping it in their basement until Marta expressed her strong displeasure with the arrangement. The morning after it was captured, Dayton told the soldiers at the base about the alligator. The soldiers tried hard to believe him, but ended up thinking this was just another of Dayton's pranks.

The alligator stayed at the Edie home only a few days until Dayton found something to put him in for a trip to the base. He then took it to Ft. Knox. The soldiers were honestly amazed when their sergeant showed up with an actual alligator.

Eventually, all the men became attached to the alligator and even built a pen for it. That alligator became the unofficial company mascot.

When each soldier had sentry duty, it was his turn to care for the alligator. The men often had to place wood in a wood burning stove next to the animal's pen. A fire had to be kept going at all times during the winter months, because if the alligator's body temperature dropped too low it would die. Dayton started to worry what he would do when the alligator grew into an adult. That concern was short lived. One night the guard on duty, who was responsible for keeping the fire going, fell asleep and let it go out.

The next morning, the other soldiers woke up to find their beloved mascot had perished. It was all Dayton could do to keep the men from seriously hurting the other soldier, who while on sentry duty had allowed the alligator to die. In their minds, the sentry had failed one of their own. Dayton got the man off base as quickly as possible. "That boy was lucky, because the other soldiers wanted to rough him up bad."

A year after purchasing their home, Dayton's father, Clarence Edie, passed away on the 6th December 1956.

Before the population exploded all around them, the area around the Edies house was desolate, overgrown pasture land used to graze cattle. There was one road leading in from a highway, and that was about it. Dayton rode the bus to his base at Ft. Knox. Dayton worked at both Ft. Knox and Ft. Bragg during his last years in the military. However, he was still sent to other bases and even foreign countries when needed. Some operations apparently took place inside the Eastern Bloc. During his lifetime, Dayton traveled to 63 countries. The country boy from Carntown, Kentucky had traveled the world as both a soldier and a spy. He faithfully served the country he loved.

This picture, taken at Fort Knox, Kentucky, October 28, 1955, shows the "alligator" with Sgt. Ambles (left), Gator (center), and Dayton (right).

Billboard at Fort Knox.

THE POST, SATURDAY, DECEMBER 15, 1956.

River Claims Ashes Of Old Fisherman

Clarence Eddie loved the Ohio River.

For most of his 77 years he had earned his living from the river, as a commercial fisherman, close to his home at Carntown, Pendleton county.

He wanted the river to claim his earthly remains. So he gave instructions to his family that when he died, he was to be cremated and his ashes scattered on the waters of the Ohio.

Mr. Eddie died unexpectedly last week. He was stricken with a heart attack while walking on Shelby street in Falmouth.

Following funeral services Monday, his body was cremated in Cincinnati.

Thursday his son, Dayton Eddie, carried out his father's wish. From a motorboat, he scattered the ashes on the water from Moscow, O., to Carntown, a distance of more than a mile.

Newspaper article, December 15, 1956.

Marching with Martin Luther King, Jr.

Dayton was promoted permanently to Master Sergeant (E-8) on 1st July 1962. The promotion took place at Gablingen Airfield in Germany. Copies of letters congratulating him on the promotion from Major General W. Paul Johnson, Colonel Edward C. Dunn, and Major General R. J. Butchers are amongst his personal papers. He also received a letter of commendation from Major Raymond A. Carlson which read in part, "Upon my departure, I want to take this opportunity to commend you for your outstanding service as Regimental Communication Chief." The Letter of Commendation goes on and on about his superior rating and work ethic while attached to the 6th Armored Cavalry at Ft. Knox, Kentucky.

There are dozens of letters of commendations within Dayton's paperwork from the 1950s and early 1960s. After reading them, it's obvious he was a soldier much admired and one his commanding officers tried to hold onto as long as possible.

Dayton once told me about one of his high-profile security assignments that really surprised me. It was 1988, and the 25th Anniversary date of the march on Washington led by Martin Luther King, Jr., and most of the front page of the newspaper that day covered the event. Dayton saw my gaze drift over the paper, and he said, "I've often wondered exactly how many people in that march were there to really support King and how many were there to watch him!"

He went on to explain that he'd been at the march on Washington, and there was good reason to think there were more people there to keep an eye on King's activities than there were to support him. At the time, every government agency was interested in what Martin Luther King was doing and what he had planned for the future. Local, state, and federal agencies were not sure what was going on inside the march, so all of them sent infiltrators to mingle with the crowd. They hoped to get any information possible and to keep things peaceful.

Agencies that were covertly represented included the FBI, CIA, and various branches of the U.S. military. There were also state and local law enforcement groups at the march. The many agencies were all there together spying on people in the march, as well as each other. Since each agency had sent covert operatives, no one knew if he was watching a King supporter or a fellow agent. Dayton knew all this because he was one of them. He said, "they" had sent him out of uniform to infiltrate the march.

The 1960s were a decade of unrest in America, when waves of riots and demonstrations swept the country. When the local authorities could not keep the peace in the inner cities and university campuses, where the disturbances were most acute, the Regular Army was brought in to contain the civil protests—and with the Army came Army Intelligence.

In carrying out this difficult mission the Army CI gained unprecedented renown within the national intelligence community, as well as federal and state law enforcement agencies.[13]

In the mid 1990s after the cold war was over and Russia's control over the Eastern Bloc countries ended, Dayton decided to take a trip with Marta to see areas that had previously been restricted. To Marta the places Dayton wanted to visit didn't seem appealing. When she asked him why he wanted to go somewhere he'd never been and knew nothing of, Dayton replied, "Says you." When Marta looked into reservations for Budapest, she asked Dayton what was there since the two of them had never been. He answered her, "Haven't I?"

Dayton was already familiar with the places they visited, proving it to Marta by acting as her tour guide on the trip. In Budapest they visited a café Dayton obviously knew well. Dayton also knew all the streets and places to go as they walked along. Dayton never explained the details. Instead he left it to us to put things together.

From official paperwork alone it is obvious that Dayton worked many operations and assignments from 1944, until his

---

[13] Sayer and Botting, *America's Secret Army*, 368

retirement in 1965. He understood at least five languages—English, Spanish, French, German, and one other, probably Italian. Several of Dayton's personal documents refer to his Cryptographic Access Authorization, being a Custodian of Cryptic Material, or of him having a TOP SECRET clearance level. There are a few documents from the 1960's within his personal papers that actually have CIC printed on them.

This photo was taken Friday, May 6, 1960. Front row, from left: M/Sgt Ethridge T. Harn, M/Sgt Cleatis L. Mullins, M/Sgt Edgar L. Kent, M/Sgt James F. Teague, M/Sgt Dayton Edie. Rear, from left: M/Sgt Herbert Tinnet, M/Sgt Robert W. Soper, M/Sgt Richard R. Gray, M/Sgt James M. Storer, M/Sgt Edward E. Harris.

Last Meeting with Dizzy Dean

Dayton had not seen his old friend Dizzy Dean in the more than 20 years since he'd enlisted in the U.S. Army. In 1964, Dean was playing golf with former President Dwight D. Eisenhower in a celebrity golf match at Southern Pines, North Carolina. That day, Dayton said Eisenhower either came real close or actually hit a hole in one.

Dayton was working out of Ft. Bragg, North Carolina, and snuck off base. Because he wasn't where he was supposed to be, Dayton didn't want to be seen, and he had to work hard to get past the secret service surrounding the former President. It was certainly a challenge for Dayton to get a message through to Dizzy Dean. It took some effort, but he finally managed to get a note past security and delivered to the old Hall of Famer that simply read, "An old friend is off in the woods."

A half hour passed after Dayton sent the message to Dizzy Dean, when he saw his old friend coming towards him. Dayton stood next to a tree, and Dizzy couldn't see who was there.

"Hum that potato down here," Dayton yelled! It was an old baseball phrase they had used years ago.

"I hear yah, but I can't see yah," Dizzy responded!

Dayton stepped out from behind the tree, so the old ball player could see him. Even though it had been over 20 years since they last seen each other, Dizzy Dean instantly recognized his old friend and cried out, "Dayton!"

The two of them enjoyed a few minutes together talking about days gone by until Dizzy remembered he had to get back to his golf game with the President. The Hall of Famer signed a golf ball and gave it to Dayton as he said goodbye. The signature read, "To an old friend — Dizzy Dean."

That meeting at Southern Pines was the last time Dayton and Dizzy Dean ever saw each other. Dean passed away 10 years later in 1974.

Dayton never came out and said it, but Dizzy Dean was his all-time favorite baseball player and a very special friend. Dayton kept a pair of cleats given to him by Dizzy Dean.

Barry Larkin, the former Cincinnati Reds short stop, was Dayton's second favorite player and his all-time favorite Reds player. If not for his gambling transgressions, Pete Rose would have held the spot as Dayton's second favorite player.

Dayton couldn't tolerate famous people who abused the public's trust. Pee Wee Reese is another player Dayton admired, especially when Reese gave Jackie Robinson his help and support, when Robinson broke the color barrier in Major League Baseball.

One Retirement Down, One to Go

In 1965 Dayton was in Berlin, Germany on his last overseas assignment. The Russians had built the wall surrounding West Berlin only four years earlier, which started the Berlin Crisis. While he was in Berlin, Dayton's childhood home of Carntown, KY was removed from the map. The small town, its buildings, structures, and houses were all moved or torn down to make room for a quarry.

Everything that wasn't destroyed was moved. Dayton never knew what happened to his Uncle John Rath's house or the boat in the basement. If Rath's house was not moved, but instead torn down, maybe the boat was finally freed from the confines of the basement and found its proper home on the water. Nothing is left in Carntown today but a rock mine. The town is gone, but Carntown still appears when you check Google Maps.

Dayton served in the United States Army from early 1943 until his retirement in 1965. Master Sergeant Dayton Edie saw combat on multiple occasions in both World War II and the Korean War. He worked covert missions and assignments during the late 1940s up to his retirement in 1965, allowing him to serve a very unique stint in the U.S. Army.

Dayton had injured others in battle and been injured himself to ensure the liberty and rights of others. In serving his country, Dayton was left with physical and mental pains that lasted the rest of his life. If you add up his accomplishments in battle, the untold number of cloak-and-dagger missions, his leadership and expertise in communications, along with all the skills and training he was able to share with others, the sum total is quite impressive. The United States of America was fortunate to be served by such a dedicated patriot.

Pictures taken the day he retired from the U.S. Army show his face both proud and sad. It is likely few people at his retirement party had any clue what Dayton had really accomplished during his military career. Dayton's official retirement from the Army was the 30th April 1965.

Dayton had served with dozens of battalions, regiments, and divisions in multiple U.S. Armies. Dayton Edie served in every Army in Europe during World War II except the Fifth Army in Italy.

He was placed in multiple units for special and various duties, many of which had to do with security, communications and radio monitoring. Master Sgt. Dayton Edie served in more units from 1943 to 1965 than anyone will ever know.

A Service Record dated 30th April 1965, has the following information listed under 'Foreign Service':

> In France 10th December 1944 through 24th April 1946.
> In Italy 22nd October 1946 through 1st June 1950
> In Korea 12th October 1952 through 24th August 1953
> In Germany 16th January 1962 through 26th December 1963

After retirement from the United States Army, Dayton Edie received several certificates of appreciation. With the passage of time more arrived, especially when his 40th and 50th anniversaries were celebrated.

Here are a few of the certificates of appreciation honoring Dayton for his service to our country:

> Freedom Team Salute Certificate of Appreciation from the United States given by Army Chief of Staff General Peter J. Schoomaker and Secretary of the Army, Francis J. Harvey.
>
> Certificate of Recognition from Pastor Dee H. Wade at the Anchorage Presbyterian Church honoring Dayton on the 11th Nov. 2007 from a proclamation by the President of the United States of America, President George W. Bush.
>
> The Battle of Normandy Foundation dedicated to honoring America's Armed Forces who fought for freedom in World War II.
>
> A U.S. flag that was flown over the United States Capitol on July 8th, 1993, requested by the Honorable Mitch McConnell, United States Senator. The flag had been flown

specifically for Dayton Edie on the occasion of the 40th reunion of the 648th Tank Destroyer Battalion. Veterans of the 648th Tank Destroyer Battalion, including Dayton were given a certificate and flag.

Wall of Liberty Official Certificate of Registration signed by Pierre Salinger, the Wall of Liberty Campaign Chairman and also a U.S. Veteran of World War II.

Once retired from the service, Dayton started a new career working at Jewish Hospital. The Hospital is located in downtown Louisville, Kentucky. After 20 years of being a soldier and spy, he turned in his cloak and dagger for a screw driver and hammer to work at a hospital. He went from being a Master Sergeant in the Army, a soldier in combat, a spy behind the Iron Curtain, and an infiltrator in the Martin Luther King, Jr. march to being a happy, humble maintenance man.

He had taken a custodial course at Ft. Knox, KY in August 1959, but I'd have to guess he never really expected to use that training.

Dayton seemed to enjoy his work at the hospital. I prefer to think of his new job as his last undercover mission, because I can guarantee you nobody at that hospital had any idea, their maintenance man was a warrior and a spy.

Eventually, Dayton accumulated enough years of service at Jewish Hospital to retire from there as well. At the end, he had two well-earned pensions from over 40 years of dedicated service.

Dayton is sitting in the bottom row, fifth from the left.

Retirement party.

Retirement party.

Retirement party.

THE WHITE HOUSE
PRESIDENT
GEORGE W. BUSH

For Immediate Release
Office of the Press Secretary
October 31, 2007

Veterans Day, 2007
A Proclamation By the President of the United States of America

Throughout our history, America has been protected by patriots who cherished liberty and made great sacrifices to advance the cause of freedom. The brave members of the United States Armed Forces have answered the call to serve our Nation, ready to give all for their country. On Veterans Day, we honor these extraordinary Americans for their service and sacrifice, and we pay tribute to the legacy of freedom and peace that they have given our great Nation.

In times of war and of peace, our men and women in uniform stepped forward to defend their fellow citizens and the country they love. They shouldered great responsibility and lived up to the highest standards of duty and honor. Our veterans held fast against determined and ruthless enemies and helped save the world from tyranny and terror. They ensured that America remained what our founders meant her to be: a light to the nations, spreading the good news of human freedom to the darkest corners of the earth.

Like the heroes before them, today a new generation of men and women are fighting for freedom around the globe. Their determination, courage, and sacrifice are laying the foundation for a more secure and peaceful world.

Veterans Day is dedicated to the extraordinary Americans who protected our freedom in years past, and to those who protect it today. They represent the very best of our Nation. Every Soldier, Sailor, Airman, Marine, and Coast Guardsman has earned the lasting gratitude of the American people, and their service and sacrifice will be remembered forever. In the words of Abraham Lincoln: " . . . let us strive on to finish the work we are in, to bind up the Nation's wounds, to care for him who shall have borne the battle . . . ." On this Veterans Day, I ask all Americans to express their appreciation to our Nation's veterans.

With respect for and in recognition of the contributions our service men and women have made to the cause of peace and freedom around the world, the Congress has provided (5 U.S.C. 6103(a)) that November 11 of each year shall be set aside as a legal public holiday to honor our Nation's veterans.

NOW, THEREFORE, I, GEORGE W. BUSH, President of the United States of America, do hereby proclaim November 11, 2007, as Veterans Day and urge all Americans to observe November 11 through November 17, 2007, as National Veterans Awareness Week. I encourage all Americans to recognize the valor and sacrifice of our veterans through ceremonies and prayers. I call upon Federal, State, and local officials to display the flag of the United States and to support and participate in patriotic activities in their communities. I invite civic and fraternal organizations, places of worship, schools, businesses, unions, and the media to support this national observance with commemorative expressions and programs.

IN WITNESS WHEREOF, I have hereunto set my hand this thirty-first day of October, in the year of our Lord two thousand seven, and of the Independence of the United States of America the two hundred and thirty-second.

GEORGE W. BUSH

Veterans Day Proclamation
by President George W. Bush, October 31, 2007.

Certificate of Recognition

A Proclamation by the President of the United States of America

Who has proclaimed November 11, 2007, as Veteran's Day and urges all Americans to observe November 11, 2007 through November 17, 2007 as National Veterans Awareness Week. He encourages all Americans to recognize the valor and sacrifice of our veterans through ceremonies and prayer.

"IN WITNESS WHEREOF, I have hereunto set my hand this thirty-first day of October, in the year of the Lord two thousand seven, and of the Independence of the United States of America the two hundred and thirty-second."

— George W. Bush —

CONGREGATIONAL PROCLAMATION

WHEREAS, You, **DAYTON EDIE**, of the UNITED STATES ARMY, have served our country during World War II; and

WHEREAS, Your self-sacrifice and determination are worthy of commendation by your neighbors and friends; and

WHEREAS, Your successful accomplishments are in keeping with the fine traditions of military service; and

WHEREAS, Your contributions have helped preserve both the freedoms promised in the Constitution of the United States, and the American way of life; therefore,

BE IT RESOLVED, that the people of Anchorage Presbyterian Church, meeting in divine worship on this 11th day of November, in the year of our Lord 2007, do herby express their deepest gratitude for your service to your country, your devotion to duty, and your faithfulness to God, by granting you this Certificate of Recognition, in the name of the Lord of light and love, the God of grace, mercy, and peace, who is the one Sovereign over all nations, and our "Captain in the well fought fight."

God bless you and your family.
God bless the "Greatest Generation", which you represent so well.
God bless our country.

Given under my hand, on Veteran's Day, 2007,
in the city of Anchorage, in the county of Jefferson,
in the Commonwealth of Kentucky, in the United States of America.

Dee H. Wade

Dee H. Wade, Pastor
Anchorage Presbyterian Church

Certificate of Recognition.

Certificate to certify that an accompanying flag
was flown over the U.S. Capitol on July 8, 1993
for the 40th reunion of the 648th Tank Destroyer Battalion.

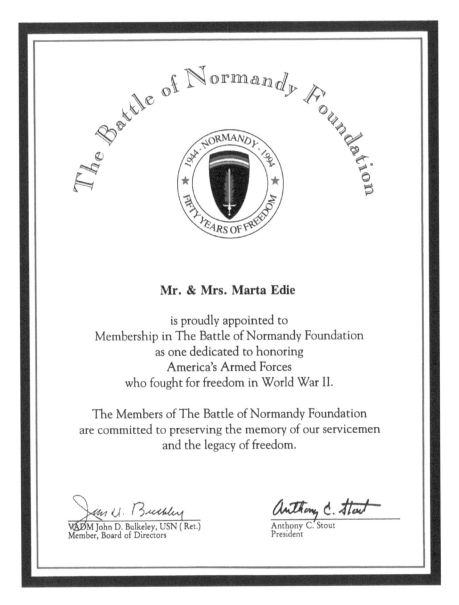

Membership certificate from The Battle of Normandy Foundation.

Certificate of Authenticity from The Battle of Normandy Foundation with a small packet of sand obtained from the beaches of Normandy.

French certificate for the 50th anniversary of the Normandy invasion.

Registration certificate for the Wall of Liberty from The battle of Normandy Foundation.

Certificate of Appreciation for service in the United States Army.

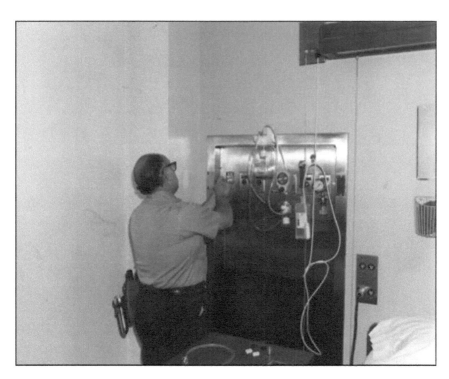

Dayton working at Jewish Hospital.

Certificate from the Kentucky Society for Hospital Engineers.

Certificate of Achievement from the Jewish Hospital in Louisville, Kentucky.

AN AMERICAN UNSUNG

Tragedy

No one should ever outlive a child. I first met Dayton in 1986 because my mother wanted me to help the Edies with their yard work. Almost as though embarrassed by how the yard was unkempt, Dayton once briefly explained why everything in his yard was so overgrown and in need of attention. "In the same year I lost a parent, my only child, and had a leg nearly cut off in an accident at work. After that year I didn't feel like doing much for about 10 years."

That year was 1976.

The parent he referred to was his mother, Lucille. She passed away from natural causes. I couldn't help but ask about his son, Michael. How had someone so young died so early? Dayton only said it was carbon monoxide poisoning and did not elaborate. My first thought was that his son might have killed himself. Since Dayton didn't want to talk about it, I never brought it up again. Years later while I was researching this book, I discovered the truth of Michael's tragic death. In the mid 1970's the Edies purchased a used car. The Edies used the bus system for their main transportation back and forth to work, and they bought the car for making weekend trips to the gated community of Doe Valley. The Edies owned four plots of land in Doe Valley, along with two mobile homes parked on the property. Dayton and Michael often went to the lake without Marta just to fish.

Doe Valley community is located about halfway between the Edie's house and Ft. Knox. When the Edies returned from their weekend trips, all of them complained of slight headaches, but they couldn't figure out the cause.

Dayton thought something might be leaking in the trailers and causing their headaches, but time passed, and he never did discover the problem.

Early one morning at their house, Dayton went to retrieve the newspaper and saw Michael sitting in the driver's seat of the car. At first, he thought nothing of it. Then he looked through the window on the driver's side door. He immediately knew Michael was gone. With his war time experience and having seen so many deaths, Dayton knew the signs a deceased body shows.

Dayton and Marta learned that the used car had a bad leak from the exhaust system. The leak had caused their headaches on the trips back and forth from Doe Valley. The family had made those trips during the summer months with the windows open for ventilation, and enough clean air had circulated through the car to keep them from being overcome by the fumes. On the October night Michael last drove the car it was cold, so he drove with the windows rolled up tight. After coming home early that morning, Michael had fallen asleep in the car and was overcome by carbon monoxide.

Dayton and Marta lost Michael on the 16th October 1976. In the Edie's basement is a furnace that burns wood, coal, or gas, and can be switched to electric. After Michael passed away, Dayton shut off the gas part of the furnace. Instead of gas, Dayton always used an electric mower to mulch the yard. He really only used his truck for picking up things like groceries and wood. When the gas water heater went bad, he replaced it with electric.

Michael.

Dayton with Michael.

The Knee Accident

An accident in 1976 nearly cut Dayton's kneecap completely off! A pane of glass had been hanging loose from a fire hose case at the hospital. The fire hose was encased in glass and hanging from the ceiling above the steps. This meant everyone had to walk under that fire hose, and if the glass part came down when someone was walking under it they could be killed.

Dayton came down the hall and noticed the glass hanging at an odd angle. No one else was around and Dayton was afraid to leave the loose glass as it was, so he reached up and pulled it with one hand hoping the glass would fall away from him. He had just lost his son Michael a month earlier, and it is likely Dayton was not in a normal frame of mind.

He had barely touched the glass when it came down slicing into his left knee. The glass cut through his kneecap, slicing it off and leaving it barely attached while it hung upside down on top of the exposed shin bone. Bleeding badly and alone, Dayton tied a tourniquet around his leg and dragged his body down a flight of stairs. At the next floor, he found a nurse who got him into a wheelchair and rushed him to the ER. Fortunately, he worked in a hospital and didn't have to go far to find a doctor.

Dayton became one of the first total knee replacement (TKR) recipients as a result of this accident. It was 1976, and the very first TKRs took place in 1974. Pain relief options have improved drastically since then, and it's still a pretty uncomfortable procedure. I can't imagine what Dayton went through over 35 years ago when they were first learning how to get patients to endure the surgery and the pain that followed.

He was lucky not to lose the leg below the knee. 1976 was not a good year for Dayton.

Dayton recovering from knee surgery.

Meeting the Edies

During the mid-1980s my Mother was designing and selling kitchens, and she happened to sell a kitchen to Dayton and Marta Edie. In the process she became close friends with them. When Marta complained about their yard needing work, Mom mentioned she had a son who worked for a landscape architect. She said on weekends and evenings, I might be able to help out.

I knew Dayton Edie had been at the Battle of the Bulge before I ever met him. I was always a huge World War II buff, so when the Edies needed yard work my mom used Dayton's military background as leverage to get me to help the couple on a regular basis. I began going to their house on weekends usually about once or twice a month. From the start no matter where we were, if Dayton Edie was talking, I was listening.

The first time I met Dayton I only knew he had fought at the Battle of the Bulge. I had been taught to always respect elders no matter what, and since Dayton was a World War II veteran, it only raised the level of my esteem. Now having said that, let me also say nothing about Dayton as an older man made me think of him as a courageous warrior. He was in his early 60s by then, and along with having acquired a slight paunch, he was bald on top and had white thinning hair on both sides. He was short and stocky, and due to his bad knee, he walked with a noticeable limp. Including the thick black-rimmed glasses he wore, nothing about Dayton indicated he had once been a battle hardened soldier.

During those first years, I also met Marta's cousin Karl Bornwasser, a former member of the Deutsches Afrika Korps. Karl and I were introduced when he came to Kentucky and stayed a few weeks with his favorite cousin. Dayton said Karl had fought in the deserts of North Africa under Field Marshall Rommel. He didn't speak much English, and I myself could make out only a little of his German. What I mainly remembered about Karl was that he was big and broad like the German soldiers Dayton spoke of often.

Karl passed away at the age of 80 in 2002.

When he was 10, Dayton paddled a small boat across the Ohio River alone to hunt persimmons. He wanted to get to the persimmons buried in the snow before the possums got them. Dayton complained that for all the work, paddling across the river, trudging through the cold, and digging through the snow the possums usually won.

As an adult, Dayton planted two persimmon trees on his property in Louisville. He first planted an American persimmon in the front yard and then a Japanese persimmon in the back yard. When the persimmons began falling Dayton was in heaven. He really loved them, always pointing one out saying, "There's a good one. Grab it before the squirrels do." Honestly, at first I couldn't stand them. Persimmons have seeds which you have to spit out. After biting into one, I sneakily tried to spit everything out when he wasn't looking!

Since he loved the fruit so much, I did not have the heart to tell him, but something in their texture nearly made me sick. We went on like that for years; him loving them and me pretending to eat them. Eventually, I ended up eating so many persimmons that I actually acquired a taste for them. If you get a good one, there is nothing better.

Even though Dayton had been considered the best shot around in his youth, his father was actually the better shot and all around hunter. After all, it was his dad who taught him to shoot, hunt, and trap. However, Clarence Edie never killed animals with a weapon. He couldn't bear to see an animal die.

Dayton's father had seen a great deal of tragedy in life, having witnessed many of his family and friends killed or hurt in mining accidents. By the time of the Depression he couldn't stand to watch an animal die, even if it was needed for food. Clarence always placed his traps along the water's edge, setting them in ways that would ensure the animal would drown before he returned.

By 1986, Dayton had become just like his dad. He could not harm or hurt anything, and he babied every critter that came his way. The many kittens and cats that found their way into his yard ended up inside the Edies house. Spiders were to be left alone the moment they ventured into Dayton's yard. The same was true of the ground squirrels that ran around tearing through his flowers.

Dayton insisted they be left alone.

Even the squirrels that came down from the trees and stole from Dayton's garden, or worse ate his beloved persimmons, were granted clemency. Dayton would shake a fist at them and threaten the squirrels, telling them he was 'going to put you in the pot,' but he never did. He waved his arms and threatened them as they ran up the trees with his fruit, but they were only empty threats. Even these cheeky bandits were to be left alone. By this stage of life Dayton wouldn't harm a fly, not even the squirrels stealing his persimmons.

With time, trust, and over the course of many conversations with him, occasionally Dayton would say something to reveal he wasn't just teaching history, but that he had been there or took part in the actual event itself. Also, the more I learned, the more it confirmed he had served in some kind of special and unique branch of the U.S. Army. Eventually, I realized my first impression of him had been way off!

It would take almost three decades along with quite a few holes dug (explained in the next chapter), to learn details and answers concerning what a fascinating life Dayton Edie lived, never mind what he did at the Battle of the Bulge. All time spent with him I will cherish forever.

Fox Holes and Cat Holes

When I first met the Edies they had six cats, but at one point there were as many as nine, and all of them lived in the house with Dayton and Marta. After I started working for Dayton, he asked me to help bury the used cat litter.

Before his knee accident Dayton had dug holes in his backyard to bury all food scraps, garbage, debris, yard waste, and cat litter the Edies accumulated over a 20 year period. He explained by saying, "The ground will take back just about anything, and generally it's good for it."

One time when the Edies went to Europe for an extended visit, I was unable to get to their house for almost four months. When they finally returned Dayton wanted a huge hole dug. After I'd dug a good-sized hole, he showed me close to a dozen five gallon buckets all covered with lids. Knowing he wanted the contents of those buckets emptied into the hole, I popped a lid off one and released a smell that could have wakened the dead.

Inside each five gallon bucket was the used, dirty cat litter that had built up over the course of those four months the Edies were in Europe. The stockpile of cat litter was in the back corner of the yard, sitting out in the summer heat waiting for me to bury it. I emptied one bucket after another into that gaping hole and covered the steaming nasty cat litter with dirt as quickly as possible. Then Dayton had me bring all the buckets to where he stored rain water to rinse them out.

"Don't want to do that to the garbage man," Dayton said with a smile.

Truth is he really loved to bury things and fill the holes.

When it came to digging those cat holes, the bigger they were, the happier Dayton was. Dayton did not find my early attempts acceptable, and I quickly found that digging a hole to Dayton's standards was no easy task. He wanted holes deep and wide enough to get your whole body into — like a military fox hole. The only difference was he called them fox holes and I called them cat holes!

After inspecting my first effort he said, "It's a good thing the Germans aren't coming at you, because that hole's barely big enough to protect your feet!" I kept digging.

The next time he came by he said, "Unlike the Battle of the Bulge, you're not dealing with frozen ground. Good thing."

I went back to digging.

Once I got the hole deep enough using a shovel, he had me to chisel it into a four sided square with a spade. By squaring off the hole, Dayton was able to maximize the space for filling.

Between what he buried from 1955 until his knee accident in 1976, and what was buried from the holes I dug added up to almost 40 years of burying stuff in his backyard. Mr. Vance, a World War II Navy Veteran who owns the house next door, says Dayton's back yard is higher than all the yards connected to it.

The Last Dates

Late in 2010 and in the heart of the winter, Dayton went into his front yard near the street. The deep ditch that used to be there had been smoothed over and covered with grass ever since city sewers were installed years before. A sign advertising a local company that had done some work for Dayton and Marta had been left on the smooth incline where the ditch used to be.

Dayton had gone outside to straighten the sign, and after leaning over to fix it, he'd lost his balance and fallen. With his bad leg and the snowy ground, he was unable to get back up. It was terribly cold and he started to worry. At one point he tried waving at passing cars. The road is rather busy, and car after car drove past as he lay there on the ground waving his arms and yelling for help.

Either no one noticed, or no one was willing to stop. Dayton started to think he might die there.

Desperate not to let that happen, he tried again to get up. This time he rolled over and positioned his body where once he was up a little, he could use his weight to pull himself up and forward. After a long struggle he finally stood.

Exhausted, he walked back to the house. He had been outside on the cold ground for close to an hour. Marta had no idea what had happened, thinking Dayton was in the garage or down in the basement all that time. Needless to say she was horrified when she heard the story.

Marta wanted Dayton to go to the hospital right then and there, but Dayton refused, saying he was fine. However, shortly after the fall he began singing and humming all the time, something he'd never done before. Marta finally insisted he go to the hospital. The doctors concluded Dayton had suffered a stroke, either before or after the fall. He did recover, getting out of the hospital and back home, even though the stroke took its toll on him.

More than a year later, Marta and Dayton stayed up late one night talking. Marta said it had been a good talk. Not that they argued all the time, but Marta said that night they had a really good conversation. After their talk, something happened she'd never seen Dayton do before. He marched into their bedroom and after coming to military attention, he barked out reveille and then said, "Edie it's time for our prayers!" Marta, lying in bed, watched him in amazement. Until that night, he had never marched, stood at attention, or displayed any military movements in front of her.

Dayton lightened the moment with a smile. The two had their nightly prayer, and went to bed. They didn't go to bed until around midnight, which was late for the Edies. They lay awake for about an hour. It was around one o'clock, and neither of them had been able to sleep. Since they couldn't sleep, Dayton asked Marta if she wanted to have some ice cream.

Marta couldn't remember the last time the two of them had eaten ice cream together, let alone at one in the morning. But the thought of having ice cream sounded good to her. Dayton and Marta both got up and ate ice cream sundaes in the wee hours of the morning. After their snack, they went back to bed.

Normally, they got up together between three and four in the morning. They rose together so they could take turns using the bathroom and watch each other so no one fell. This night, Marta went first and as usual went back to bed. She watched Dayton get up and head to the restroom. When he came back, instead of going to bed, he headed off to the kitchen. A few minutes passed and Dayton had not returned. Hearing nothing, Marta decided to go see what he was doing.

She found him at the dining room table. Dayton was sitting there eating an orange. Marta sat with him and shared the orange. They talked about how fruits had gone up in price but down in taste.

Between the ice cream and the orange, Dayton and Marta had enjoyed two unexpected early morning dates. They finished the orange, and after more talking, they went back to bed.

A few hours later at seven o'clock, Marta woke and noticed Dayton was still sleeping. She chalked it up to his insomnia from the night before. Normally, Dayton was the early bird and first to rise. She could see him sleeping on his side and resting on his good ear which meant he couldn't hear her. Usually, that was a sign he was deep in sleep. Marta left him alone and went to make coffee.

Dayton was still not up when the coffee finished brewing. Most days the smell of fresh-brewed coffee would have him out of bed, so Marta grew concerned. Marta went to the bedroom to check on Dayton and tell him coffee was ready. She found him still in bed, not responding to her calls. After the two of them had gone to bed early that day, Dayton Edie's heart had failed. He had passed in his sleep.

Family friend, Mike Lowery arrived Saturday morning to do yard work I had stopped doing long ago due to knee issues, only to find police cars in the driveway. Mike thought maybe there had been a break-in since the police arrived before the ambulance. When the female coroner arrived, she asked Mike to stay with Marta in case she forgot anything they said. The coroner's opinion was Dayton's heart had failed but that he had not suffered. They knew he had gone peacefully because there was no strain on his face or rings around the eyes. Dayton Edie had passed peacefully in his sleep.

Pastor Dee H. Wade, Dayton's friend and pastor, told those who gathered for his memorial that since he had passed in his sleep and hadn't suffered, "It had been a good death." Before his passing, Dayton had given Marta a special last night together and something for her to hold onto until they were together again.

Dayton Edie passed on January 7th, 2012. His memorial was held on February 9th, the 87th anniversary of his birth.

Dayton Edie.

Excuses and Explanations

When Dayton passed, I was recovering from knee replacement surgery and off work with little to do except my physical therapy. It freed up my time to work on a speech for Dayton's memorial.

Almost ten years had passed since I had worked for him. Dayton was unaware of my bad knees, until just after the surgery and right before his death. Prior to reaching a point where I could no longer work at all for Dayton, if the knees flared up to force a cancellation I always made up an excuse. Not wishing to worry Dayton of my knee problems I never told him the truth of why I couldn't work. Once, after cancelling a visit at the last minute, he said, "Boy you got more excuses than Carter had liver pills."

Dayton had actually called a few days after I got home from surgery to check on me. Due to my knee replacement he said, "Now you're a club member." That ended up being the last time we spoke.

All this was written in the hopes that Dayton Edie is never forgotten. He never once bragged about doing his duty. He rarely gave details, revealing various stories to a single person at a time, and then usually only telling that story once. I was fortunate to know the people closest to him who were willing to share the stories they had heard when they learned I was compiling his biography.

Dayton Edie is a true American hero. I occasionally asked if he would let me contact somebody about his actions at the Battle of the Bulge, such as a historian, a fellow veteran, somebody in the media, or anybody who could help Dayton get the accolades he so richly deserved. But when I asked, he always said no, not to bother. Dayton was content with the nicknames he'd been given by his fellow soldiers - The Professor and The Stacker. These terms of admiration were sufficient for the humble country boy from Kentucky.

If his story reaches the public, it is my hope a veteran still remembers him from that time and will come forward; if not a veteran from World War II, maybe someone from Korea, the OSS or

CIC. Veterans from World War II are disappearing fast - over 600 a day, so official recognition of Dayton's deeds at the Battle of the Bulge will probably never happen, but you and I will know the truth, and that will be enough.

Without the help and information from my wonderful mom, Pat Finley, and friends like Mike Lowery, Matthew Lynn, Mark Hatchel, Leon Embry, Janet Bell, and many others this book would never have been published.

Professor Dan Lawrence (Oklahoma University) helped with early advice and suggestions, followed later with much needed help in editing.

Dayton's biography was compiled from official documents from the National Archives, Dayton's personal papers, stories he told others, and my own conversations with the man. Finding the answers to complete his history has been like completing a puzzle—not always easy, but very, very rewarding.

My wife Susan, stepson Michael Littlefield, and stepdaughter Kristy Littlefield Oiler were all instrumental in helping make this book happen long before the first word was written.

This book was authorized by Marta Edie. She agreed Dayton should be remembered and honored. Marta Edie has my deepest appreciation for giving me authorization and access to Dayton's papers and for outright giving most of them to me for this book. Like Dayton, Marta had no regrets, but there were difficult times. Marta endured the horrible loss of Michael's passing. With Dayton's passing, Marta soldiered on, but with a heavy heart.

Mike Lowery was instrumental in learning several details that were previously unknown, and he wrote the following for his friend Dayton:

Here's to you old friend
May our paths cross again
Where tomatoes and flowers and cold beer prevails

Special thanks must be given to Jonathan Fletcher for his recording of Dayton in 2011, which clarified a number of issues. Jonathan recorded Dayton for two hours as he spoke about Wobbelin and many other things concerning his service in World War II.

The military poems in the book were two of Dayton's personal favorites. After sending an email to George L. Skypeck, he personally responded and gave me permission to use his poem, which was a great honor. He basically said, "Do the veteran proud."

I read a short speech at Dayton's memorial. After reading the speech about Dayton, a man many at the memorial had known for decades, these same people were surprised and thrilled to learn the few tidbits of information revealed of him. I realized I needed not just to write a speech but to tell the world the entire story about Dayton Edie. As was the case so many times in our friendship, Dayton gave me something I will treasure forever: the opportunity to share his story with the world. I can only hope to do that story justice.

Let this be a salute to a great man. May you rest in peace, Mr. Edie.

On June 18th, 2013, a small ceremony took place at Arlington National cemetery to honor Dayton Edie. His ashes were returned to the earth, and a marker was placed there for him. The marker is for his service in the Korean War and acknowledges he earned the Bronze Star and Purple Heart there. It's a lovely marker, but the engraver put the wrong birth date on the stone, and there is nothing on it acknowledging his service during World War II. Until that marker is corrected, Dayton Edie will truly remain An American Unsung.

Marta Liesel Edie passed away 10 July 2016. Just as her beloved Dayton had four and half years earlier, Marta died peacefully in their home.

Medals and Honors

Official U.S. Military documentation verifies Dayton Edie was the recipient of the following medals and awards:

The Bronze Star Medal
The Purple Heart
The Korean Service Medal with three Bronze Service Stars
The Combat Infantry Badge
The United Nations Service Medal
The National Defense Service Medal
The Good Conduct Medal with seven loops
The European Theater Ribbon with two Bronze stars
The World War II American Campaign Medal
The World War II Victory Medal
The Army of the Occupation Medal
A Presidential Testimonial
The Army Commendation Ribbon with metal pendant
Republic of Korea Presidential Unit Citation

Battalions, Divisions, and HQs Dayton Served

Here are some of the units, camps, forts, and headquarters Dayton served:

605th Tank Destroyer Battalion
628th Tank Destroyer Battalion
644th Tank Destroyer Battalion
648th Tank Destroyer Battalion
653rd Tank Destroyer Battalion
655th Tank Destroyer Battalion
704th Tank Destroyer Battalion
705th Tank Destroyer Battalion
805th Tank Destroyer Battalion
17th Airborne Division
18th Airborne Corps
82nd Airborne Infantry
45th Infantry Division (179th Infantry)
179th Infantry Regiment
Camp Hood, Texas
Camp Atterbury, Indiana
Camp Stoneman, California
Reception Center 3431 ASU Ft. Jackson, South Carolina
OAB 6901 ASU California
2nd Infantry Division
6th Infantry Division
8th Infantry Division
70th Infantry Division
79th Infantry Division
84th Infantry Division
88th Infantry Division
24th Infantry Division APO 112
1st Armored Division
2nd Armored Division

3rd Armored Division
16th Cavalry Regiment
11th Armored Cavalry Regiment
6th Armored Cavalry Regiment
9th Cavalry Regiment
22nd Tank Company
18th Signal Service Company (Trieste, Free Territory of Trieste)
2nd Battle Group 19th Infantry Regiment
50th Signal Battalion (Corps)
66th Signal Battalion Ft. Bragg, North Carolina
6th Armored Cavalry Ft. Knox, Kentucky
2nd Training Regiment Armor Ft. Knox, Kentucky
European Constabulary
Armored Forces Headquarters
United States Army Training Center USATC Armor
U.S. Army Armor School
U.S. Army Signal Corps
Supreme Headquarters Allied Expeditionary Force SHAEF
Headquarters U.S. Army Center Ft. Knox, Kentucky
Headquarters Frankfurt, Germany Military Post APO 757
Headquarters Oakland Army Base California
Headquarters 6th Armored Cavalry
Headquarters 373rd Transport Battalion Camp Stoneman, California
Headquarters 19th Infantry
Headquarters 24th Infantry Division
Headquarters 3rd Howitzer Battalion 16th Artillery
Headquarters Trieste APO 209
Headquarters Camp Drake Rd APO 613
Headquarters Ft. Dix, New Jersey
Headquarters Tank Destroyer School Camp Hood, Texas
Headquarters 2D Battle Group 19th Infantry APO 112
Headquarters General Depot 7178 APO 209
Headquarters 88th Infantry Division APO 88
Headquarters 7th Artillery, Augsburg, Germany
54th Artillery Group at Ft. Bragg, North Carolina
509th Tank Battalion
740th Tank Battalion
741st Tank Battalion

1st Army
2nd Army
3rd Army
5th Army
6th Army
7th Army
8th Army
9th Army
10th Army Corp
7th Armor (The Lucky 7th)
U.S. Army 1st Corps
3rd Infantry
38th Armored Infantry

Special Orders and Security Clearances

1940s

Special orders number 235. Headquarters, Tank Destroyer School at Camp Hood, Texas. Restricted material dated 1st October 1943. Pvt. Dayton Edie (35795310) is in the 655th Tank Destroyer Battalion. The School was under the command of Colonel Paul M. Martin, Cavalry Executive, and signed by 1st Lt. William R. Bowdoin. Including Dayton there are three other soldiers from the 655th Tank Destroyer Battalion listed on this form. The rest of the soldiers are from various other battalions, indicating they possibly all had been chosen or volunteered for special training of some kind.

Recertified Corrected Copy training and the dates they took place, dated 3rd October 1944. Day and night infiltration training are written in the document.

Separation qualification record. A summary of Dayton's time during the military occupation, dated 30th April 1946. This form notes that during the occupation Dayton was a Telephone Operator and he "Served for seventeen months in the European Theater of Operations with Company A, 605th Tank Destroyer Battalion, operated a telephone switchboard to relay incoming or outgoing messages in a German town of twenty thousand people. Made connections with outside lines for outgoing messages, manipulated keys and cords to receive incoming calls and to make connections."

Soldiers qualification card. With Dayton having qualified in 1945 as both a heavy machine gun operator and a telephone operator, dated 16th May 1949.

Enlisted record and report of separation. Trust at the top of document, along with information that he was the message center clerk while stationed in Trieste, Free Territory of Trieste, dated 16th May 1949.

Service record. Consists of ten pages, dated 16th May 1949. Within the ten pages can be found "Trust, PBI (Cryptographic) completed on 4th April 1949" and "report filed G-2 HQ Trust on 1st March 1949."

Special order number 133. Restricted material, dated 9th June 1949. This document pertains to Dayton's promotion to sergeant under the command of Major General Hoge, Colonel John L. Whitelaw, and signed by Captain Harry W. Roberts.

Authorization for regimental or unit mail clerk certificate-Frankfurt, Germany, dated 15th September 1949.

1950s

Soldier's qualification card indicating Dayton was a Central Office Telephone Switchboard Operator, dated 28th February 1951.

Provisions as to membership or association with certain organizations form-part of a loyalty certificate, dated 17th May 1952. "Consolidated list of organizations designated by the Attorney General on October 30, 1950, pursuant to Executive order No. 9835" is on the document with a list of groups considered fascist, communist, totalitarian, and/or subversive, along with, "Organizations which have adopted a policy of advocating or approving the commission of acts of force and violence to deny others their rights under the Constitution of the United States."

Another page has a list of, "Organizations which seek to alter the form of government of the United States by unconstitutional means."

Security information, restricted material with (pipeline) on it, dated 25th October 1952.

Qualification record indicating Dayton was a Signal Clerk and Field wireman dated 20th October 1953.

Special orders number 212. Headquarters 45th Infantry Division, sending Dayton and other soldiers of the 179th Infantry 45th Infantry Division to Pusan redeployment depot, dated 31st July 1953.

Special orders number 254. Headquarters, Ft. Jackson, South Carolina dated 30th Oct. 1953. By order of Lieutenant Colonel Hinson, Major E. A. Warner, and signed by Thomas O. Deer CMO USA Asst. Adj.

Assignment memorandum. Headquarters, Ft. Bragg, North Carolina dated 5th November 1953. By command of Major General Cleland, Colonel Harvey Shelton, and signed by Billy C. Allen, CWO USA Asst. Adj.

Special orders number 222. Headquarters, Ft. Knox, Kentucky dated 19th September 1955.

Special orders number 115. Headquarters Ft. Knox, Kentucky dated 15th May 1956. This document has G2 next to his assignment.

Special orders number 167. Headquarters, Ft. Knox, Kentucky dated 16th July 1956. This document refers to Dayton being part of a Signal Instruction Team consisting of four soldiers.

Special orders number 149. Headquarters, Ft. Knox, Kentucky dated 1st July 1957.

Special orders number 155. Headquarters, Ft. Knox, Kentucky dated 23rd June 1959.

1960s

Enlisted qualification record, G2, Trust, and Top Secret printed on it, dated 9th May 1960.

Certificate of clearance and/or security determination under EO 10450, Ft. Knox, Kentucky dated 27th May 1960. This document indicates the Highest Classification or Type of Information to which access is authorized in the order of Top Secret, Secret, Confidential or Cryptologic Duties. Dayton Edie was authorized the highest level of Top Secret. It was signed by Orrin A. Roach (Civ.).

Special orders number 170. Headquarters, Ft. Knox, Kentucky U.S. Army Armor Center dated 26th July 1960. This document has CIC printed on it.

Inspection of crypto facility. Headquarters, Ft. Knox, Kentucky armor Center, dated 10th March 1961. Crypto to security officer and registered Crypto material is printed on this document.

Special orders number 255. Headquarters, Ft. Knox, Kentucky dated 24th Nov. 1961. This document has CIC on it twice, and one of the two times directly relates to Dayton.

Cryptographic access authorization, briefing and debriefing certificate issued to Dayton, 2nd September 1963.

Cryptographic access authorization, briefing, and debriefing certificate issued to Dayton, 13th December 1963.

Armed forces security questionnaire signed by Dayton and witnessed by Major Charles D. Smith, dated January 1964.

Special order number 42. Ft. Bragg, North Carolina, 54th Artillery Group, dated 18th March 1964. Crypto and Top Secret are printed on this document and signed by Major Charles D. Smith.

Cryptographic access authorization, briefing, and debriefing certificate issued to Dayton, dated 26th April 1964.

Special order number 128. Headquarters, Ft. Bragg, North Carolina, dated 11th September 1964. Commo Security Equip OP School on document signed by Major Charles D. Smith.

Security clearance certificate. Headquarters, Ft. Bragg, North Carolina, dated 11th September 1964. "This is to certify that M/Sgt. Dayton Edie, EA-35795310, has a Top Secret Cryptic Access Security Clearance" and signed by Captain Cromwell D. ST. Clair, Jr. Group G2.

Special order number 162. Headquarters, 54th Artillery Group, Ft. Bragg, North Carolina 28307 dated 13th November 1964.

Special order number 105. from the Department of Army, Washington D. C., dated 19th April 1965. This form approves Master Sgt. Edie's upcoming retirement set for 1st May 1965. Made official by Major General J. C. Lambent and General Harold K. Johnson, Chief of Staff and signed by 2nd Lt. Christopher S. Carlson. CIC is printed on this document.

Enlisted qualification record referring to Dayton Edie as a Wireman, communications center specialist and a senior communications instructor, dated 30th April 1965. Also BI, Trust, SPH, and Top Secret appear on this form.

Service records of Dayton Edie, dated 30th April 1965. This document has a lot of general information, along with exact dates and departures including those to Korea and back. There is also verification of his records within this document, including paperwork for World War II medals, proving Dayton Edie participated in World War II.

Special order number 304. Headquarters, 24th Infantry Division, APO 112 U S Forces, dated 11th November 1963. From the Commander: Colonel B. M. Read and signed by 2nd Lt. R. S. Tucker. CIC appears on this document, along with Munich and Augsburg Units and relate directly to orders for Sgt. Dayton Edie.

Taylor informed Lieutenant Colonel Dale M. Garvey, the commander of CIC Region IV (Munich-Augsburg), and both agreed that in spite of Barbie's 'wanted' status he could prove a valuable tool in the intelligence war against the Soviets in Germany.[14]

"Barbie" refers to former Gestapo member Klaus Barbie nicknamed the Butcher of Lyon.

---

[14] Sayer and Botting, *America's Secret Army*, 324

Physical Examination and Induction, 23 February 1943.

```
                          HEADQUARTERS
                        24TH INFANTRY DIVISION
                        APO 112  US FORCES

SPECIAL ORDERS
NUMBER    304              EXTRACT              11 November 1963

        11. TC 246. Fol rsg dir eff on EDCSA. Indiv will rept as indic for trans
to CONUS and/or further asg. WP TDN TPA in CONUS. 2142010 01-1661-1663-1667
21516 S99-999. CIC for EM: 2 4 1 A 03. Shpmt of POV & HHG auth.

EDIE, DAYTON  RA35795310  MSGT E8 312.00  HHB 2d Bn 7th Arty APO 112 NY NY
  Rept to: USEUCOM Aerial Port of Emb Rhein/Main AB Frankfurt Ger
  Asg to:  54th Fld Arty Gp HHB Ft Bragg NC
  Rept date(trans): 30 Dec 63
  DOR: 1 May 60   HOR: NA   Temp adrs: Valley Station Ky
  Mo OS(cur tour): 36 (NT 36)   Lv data: Thirty (30) DDALV
  PCS(MDC): RD   Auth: DA Msg 70910 EPADS-C 14 Aug 63 cited in AEAAG-PM
  Tvl data: Air trans auth. AMD for EM: FRF-WRI-3PC-5506-AZ. Auth bag alws
            for mil pers 66 lbs. Flt Nr: G-022
  ADC: 3 yrs   Comp: RA   BASD: 1 Apr 43
  BPED: 1 Apr 43   ETS: 16 Feb 66   EDCSA: 0 Jan 64
  Sp instr: Pers rec WB proc UP USAREUR Reg 614-50 prior to dprt fr home sta
            & will acmp indiv during tvl. Indiv will undergo med insp immed
            prior to dprt fr home sta & WBI proper med cert. Imm rqr of
            AR 40-562 WB complied w/prior to dprt fr unit. Indiv will sbm
            req for pay action to arrive at PSD 20 days prior to port call
            date for Munich units and 15 days prior to port call date for
            Augsburg units, if payment is auth. If indiv debarks at a point
            in the New York area not manned by a USA Returnee-Reassignment
            Team, he w/contact the USA Reassignment Station, Ft Hamilton NY.
            Contact WB made only by phone (SH 5-7900, ext 22223) and not in
            person. Alcoholic beverages not permitted aboard MATS aircraft.

        FOR THE COMMANDER:

OFFICIAL:
                                       B. M. READ
                                       Colonel, GS
                                       Chief of Staff
    R S Tucker
    R. S. TUCKER
    2d Lt, AGC
    Asst AG

DISTRIBUTION:
35 - 35 ea indiv conc/1/
40 - Composite Team 7
 2 - CO, HHB 2d Bn 7th Arty APO 112
 5 - CO, 54th Fld Arty Gp HHB Ft Bragg NC
20 - PSD ATTN: SO Team
 1 - G-1, 24th Inf Div APO 112
 5 - Billeting Off ATTN: Central Clearance APO 178

SPECIAL DISTRIBUTION:
 1 - Dir. EPD ORO ATTN: EPECD Wash 25 DC
```

Munich and Augsburg units document, 11 November 1963.

```
                              R E S T R I C T E D
WP  - Will proceed to
TDN - Travel directed is necessary in the military service
IGF - It being impracticable for the Govt to furn rations in kind and/or qrs
UP  - Under the provisions of
                              HEADQUARTERS
                           TANK DESTROYER SCHOOL
                            CAMP HOOD, TEXAS

SPECIAL ORDERS)                                            1 Oct 1943

NUMBER    235)              E X T R A C T

     1.  Fol EM having completed the course of instruction in Enlisted Weapons
#49 Stu Regt TD Sch are reld fr temp dy thereat and WP orgn indicated. Asteri:
(*) indicates non-graduates. TDN. IGF while traveling each EM will be furn
meal tickets for the no of meals indicated UP AR 30-2215. 1-5200 P 432-02 A
0425-24. Govt motor T will be utilized in the case of orgn sta at Cp Hood
and North Cp Hood. Auth AR 350-110. UP AR 615-25 an appropriate entry will
be made under item "Service Schools" on each sol Qualification Card WD AGO
Form #20.
                         To Cp Hood Texas
Cpl Howard G Winker 37156925                        603 TD Bn
Pvt Dayton Edie 35795310                            655 TD Bn
Pvt Linus D Rehmel 35098109                         655 TD Bn
Cpl Paul Stofleth 39286384                          655 TD Bn
Pvt Robert J Austin 35052045                        656 TD Bn
Pvt Harold L Drawn 35053546                         656 TD Bn
Pvt James W Duffy 39041220                          656 TD Bn
Pfc George F Baker 33629231                         658 TD Bn
Pfc Erwin F Junk 36815448                           658 TD Bn
Pfc Doleslaw S Mudro 36591642                       658 TD Bn
Pfc Henry V Wynicki 36591717                        658 TD Bn
Pfc Harold T Yctke 36592367                         658 TD Bn
Cpl Richard J Prohaska 35319782                     692 TD Bn
Techn Gr V Fred L Cesaris 35398407                  801 TD Bn
Cpl Earl J Kennedy 34142032                         801 TD Bn
                      To North Cp Hood Texas
S/Sgt Linzie J Crowder 17027255                     649 TD Bn
Cpl Fred R Hamilton 37517662                        649 TD Bn
Cpl Johnnie W Johnson Jr 37608736                   649 TD Bn
Techn Gr V Lincoln Mackey 37517458                  649 TD Bn
Pvt Robert J Robinson 32162194                      795 TD Bn
Cpl Mosca C Tindle 18086770                         795 TD Bn
Sgt Leonard H McGavock Jr 20621276                  795 TD Bn
                    To Cp Young California (7 meals)
Sgt Jack R McDonnell 39093700 (in ch)               607 TD Bn
Techn Gr V Hugh H Tucker 35719889                   607 TD Bn
Pfc Delbert R Bundschuh 35538992                    811 TD Bn
Pfc Floyd E Furden 35679705                         811 TD Bn
Cpl Albert J Hanrahan 35679551                      811 TD Bn
Pfc Eugene Jones 35355796                           811 TD Bn
Cpl Charles G Smith 35578459                        811 TD Bn
                    To Cp Rucker Alabama (6 meals)
Pfc Harvey W Baxter 34588728                        630 TD Bn
Pfc John P Lengyel 33161589                         630 TD Bn
Sgt William R Morgan 33161542 (in ch)               630 TD Bn
Cpl James M McFeeley 33161581                       630 TD Bn
Pfc Louie K Peavy 34682162                          630 TD Bn
Pfc Theodore . Clough 31175793                      804 TD Bn
```

Restricted document, Camp Hood, Texas, 1 October 1943.

HEADQUARTERS 82ND AIRBORNE DIVISION
OFFICE OF THE DIVISION COMMANDER

APO 469, in the Field
7 February 1945.

SUBJECT: Letter of Appreciation.

TO : Commanding Officer, 740th Tank Battalion.

1. I would like to express to you my appreciation for the splendid performance of your battalion during its period of attachment to this division. During that time the division, with your able assistance, has participated in the attack to pinch off the ARDENNES salient, destroying the 62d Volks Grenadier Division. Following that, it has advanced into Germany to the east, penetrating the SIEGFRIED Line and seizing the key defenses at UDENBRETH. These accomplishments were only possible with the courageous and zealous assistance of the personnel of your battalion. Their esprit and elan have been the subject of much favorable comment by all members of the division. It has been a pleasure and a privilege to have had you serve with us and I sincerely hope that the fortunes of war will bring us together once again. I am proud to have served with such fine soldiers.

JAMES M. GAVIN,
Major General, U. S. Army,
Commanding.

Letter of Recognition, 740th Tank Battalion, 7 February 1945.

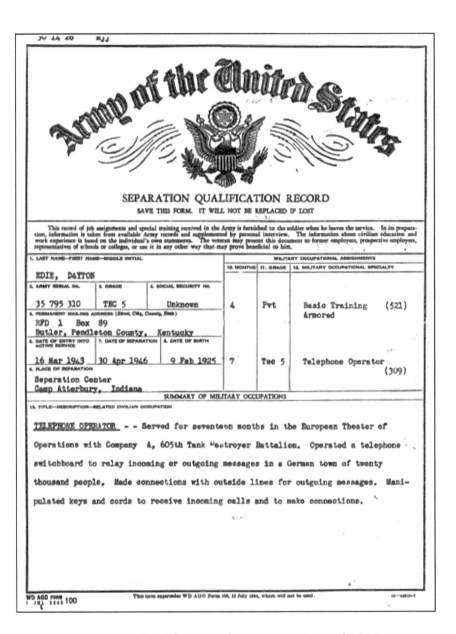

Separation Qualification document, 30 April 1946.

Separation Qualification document, 30 April 1946.

EDIE DAYTON

To you who answered the call of your country and served in its Armed Forces to bring about the total defeat of the enemy, I extend the heartfelt thanks of a grateful Nation. As one of the Nation's finest, you undertook the most severe task one can be called upon to perform. Because you demonstrated the fortitude, resourcefulness and calm judgment necessary to carry out that task, we now look to you for leadership and example in further exalting our country in peace.

Harry Truman

THE WHITE HOUSE

Presidential letter thanking Dayton for his service, 1945.
These were printed by the hundreds of thousands
With only the service member's name added.

PROVISIONS AS TO MEMBERSHIP IN OR ASSOCIATION WITH CERTAIN ORGANIZATIONS

Associations which may be considered as establishing reasonable grounds for invoking appropriate penalties include but are not limited to membership in, affiliation with, or sympathetic association with, any foreign or domestic organization, association, movement, group or combination of persons having the following characteristics:

1. Which practices, seeks to practice, or advocates either:
   (a) Denial, to any person, group of persons, or class of persons within the United States or territory subject to its jurisdiction, of any right or rights which the Federal Constitution guarantees or protects against encroachment by either or both Federal and State Governments when such denial is attempted by force, violence, or intimidation, or

   (b) Alteration of the existing form of government of the United States or territory subject to its jurisdiction, or of the existing economic, social, or political order within it when such alteration is through or with the aid of force, violence, or intimidation.

2. Which is disclosed by investigation, or is designated by the Attorney General of the United States to be totalitarian, fascist, communist, or subversive, or as having adopted a policy of advocating or approving the commission of acts of force or violence to deny persons their rights under the Constitution of the United States, or as seeking to alter the form of government of the United States by unconstitutional means regardless of practice, advocacy, or non-advocacy of any of the tenets set forth in 1 (a) and 1 (b) above.

I certify, as regards membership in or association with certain organizations, that:

1. I have read the instructions on the use of this form and understand them.
2. I have read the provisions applying to membership in or association with certain organizations and I understand them.
3. I have read, and so signified by signing, the attached list of organizations, associations, movements, groups, and combinations of persons listed on this form.
4. I have entered in the table below the name(s) of the organization(s) shown on the attached list with which I am or have been associated in any of the following respects:
   (a) I am or have been a member.
   (b) I am or have been employed.
   (c) I have attended or been present at formal or informal meetings or gatherings.

(d) I have attended, been present at, or engaged in, organizational or social activities or activities which they sponsored.
(e) I have sold, given away, or distributed written, printed, or otherwise recorded matter published by them.
(f) I have been identified or associated in some other manner.

5. If I have had no such associations, I have so indicated by writing "None" or "None to my knowledge" in the table below.
6. I understand that if what I state below is found to be incorrect, incomplete, or misleading in any important particular, I may be subject to prosecution and punishment under the appropriate laws of the United States.
7. I understand the meaning of the statements made in the certifications above.

Name of Organization	Currently a Member		Formerly a Member		Dates of Membership		Location of Membership
	Yes	No	Yes	No	From—	To—	
none							

Statement as to certification of membership in or association with certain organizations. (For each name entered in the table above, set forth a detailed account of the nature and extent of association with, and activities in connection with, each organization indicated, including dates, places, and precise description of credentials now or formerly held. Use the space provided below and attach as many extra sheets as necessary for this purpose.)

not to my knowledge.

Given under my hand this _____ day of _____ 19__

Signature of Witnessing Officer _____   Signature of Person Making Certification _____

Security and Loyalty certificate.

Security and Loyalty certificate.

IV.—QUESTIONS

(For each answer checked "Yes" under question 2, set forth a full explanation under "Remarks" below)

Question	YES	NO
1. I have read the list of names of organizations, groups, and movements set forth under Part II of this form and the explanation which precedes it.	yes	
2. Concerning the list of organizations, groups and movements set forth under Part II above:		
a. Are you now a member of any of the organizations, groups, or movements listed?		no
b. Have you ever been a member of any of the organizations, groups, or movements listed?		no
c. Are you now employed by any of the organizations, groups, or movements listed?		no
d. Have you ever been employed by any of the organizations, groups, or movements listed?		no
e. Have you ever attended any meeting of any of the organizations, groups, or movements listed?		no
f. Have you ever attended any social gathering of any of the organizations, groups, or movements listed?		no
g. Have you ever attended any gathering of any kind sponsored by any of the organizations, groups, or movements listed?		no
h. Have you prepared material for publication by any of the organizations, groups, or movements listed?		no
i. Have you ever corresponded with any of the organizations, groups, or movements listed or with any publication thereof?		no
j. Have you ever contributed money to any of the organizations, groups, or movements listed?		no
k. Have you ever contributed services to any of the organizations, groups, or movements listed?		no
l. Have you ever subscribed to any publication of any of the organizations, groups, or movements listed?		no
m. Have you ever been employed by a foreign government or any agency thereof?		no
n. Are you now a member of the Communist Party of any foreign country?		no
o. Have you ever been a member of the Communist Party of any foreign country?		no
p. Have you ever been the subject of a loyalty or security hearing?		no
q. Are you now or have you ever been a member of any organization, association, movement, group or combination of persons not on the Attorney General's list which advocates the overthrow of our constitutional form of government, or which has adopted the policy of advocating or approving the commission of acts of force or violence to deny other persons their rights under the Constitution of the United States, or which seeks to alter the form of government of the United States by unconstitutional means?		no
r. Have you ever been known by any other last name than that used in signing this questionnaire?		no

REMARKS

none to my knowledge D.E.

Page 3

Security and Loyalty certificate.

LOYALTY CERTIFICATE FOR PERSONNEL OF THE ARMED FORCES

INSTRUCTIONS ON THE USE OF THIS FORM

The Department of Defense has the authority to establish and promulgate detailed procedures to implement the national policy relating to loyalty of persons entering on duty with the Armed Forces. This has been determined by appropriate authority to include restrictions as to membership in or association with certain organizations and of certain standards of conduct. If Federal Constitutional Privilege against self-crimination; i. e., the making of a statement which will expose you to criminal trial, is claimed about all or any part of any conduct, membership, or association in question you may so claim by stating in the space indicated "Federal Constitutional Privilege is Claimed" or "Federal Constitutional Privilege is Claimed as to ....," describing the specific part of any conduct, membership, or association about which claim is made.

Concealment of, misrepresentation as to, or failure to divulge in full, conduct or associations of the character set forth in the provisions, at the time of execution of these certificates in any component of the Department of Defense may constitute grounds for discharge, separation, or other disposition of personnel, and action shall be taken by the Armed Forces for causing trial before a general court martial, or the facts will be made known to appropriate civil authorities, as the law may provide in such cases. Upon indication that any person has misrepresented, concealed, or failed to divulge in full previous conduct or associations of the character set forth, the Service having responsibility thereof shall take appropriate action.

Consequently, you must read the following provisions as to membership in or association with certain organizations and as to standards of conduct very carefully and be sure you understand them. If there is anything which you do not understand in either of these sets of provisions or in the certifications to be made, ask a commissioned officer to explain them to you. When you are certain that you understand both the provisions and the certificates, complete the certificates and sign them in the presence of a witnessing officer. Penalties for making a false statement may be very severe.

PROVISIONS AS TO STANDARDS OF CONDUCT

1. Conduct which may be considered as establishing reasonable grounds for invoking appropriate penalties shall include, but is not limited to, one or more of the following:

(*a*) Sabotage, espionage, or attempts or preparations therefor, or intimate and sympathetic associations with or voluntary assistance to persons who the subject of investigation has reasonable cause to believe may be spies or saboteurs.

(*b*) Treason, sedition, or writings and acts which can reasonably be considered as intended to encourage seditious or treasonable opinions or actions.

(*c*) Advocacy of revolution or of force or violence to alter the existing constitutional form of government of the United States; advocacy of revolution or of force or violence to bring about economic, political, or social change.

(*d*) Intentional unauthorized disclosure to any person under circumstances which may indicate disloyalty to the United States, of documents or information of a classified or nonpublic character.

(*e*) Acting, attempting to act, or knowingly failing to act when such conduct is calculated to serve the interests of another government in preference to the interests of the United States of America.

I certify, as regards the standards of conduct, that:

1. I have read the instructions on the use of this form and I understand them.

2. I have read the provisions applying to the standards of conduct and I understand them.

3. If I have engaged in any such conduct, I have so indicated by describing in the statement below the nature thereof.

4. If I have not engaged in any such conduct, I have so indicated by writing "None" or "None to my knowledge" in the statement below.

5. I understand that if what I state below is found to be incorrect, incomplete, or misleading in any important particular, I may be subject to prosecution and punishment under the appropriate laws of the United States.

6. I understand the meaning of the statements made in the certifications above.

Statement as to certification of conduct (*Attach additional sheets if necessary for a full, detailed statement*):

Typed Full Name of Person Making Certification	Service No. (If any)	Status for Which Being Considered (e. g., Com. O., WO., Enl. ROTC affiliation, etc.)
Dayton Edie	RA35795310	Enlisted Personnel

Station to Which Certification Submitted	Typed Name and Grade of Witnessing Officer
Oakland Army Base, Oakland 14, California	HOWARD F. STEINFELD, Captain

DD FORM 1 APR 50 98 — Replaces NME Form 98, 1 Oct 48, which is obsolete.

Security and Loyalty certificate.

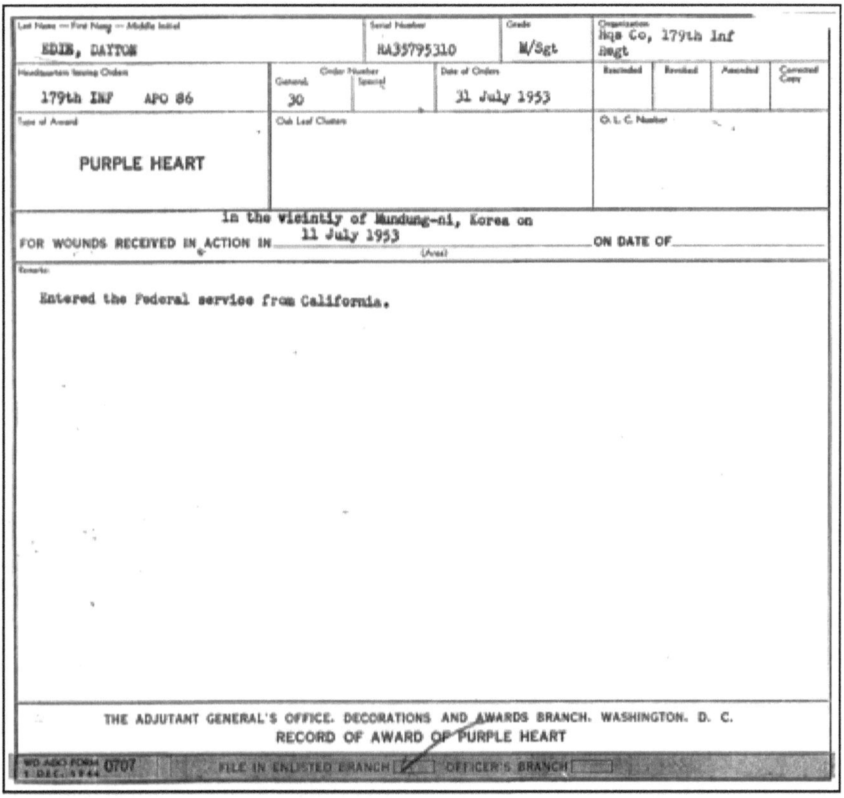

Last Name — First Name — Middle Initial	Serial Number	Grade	Organization
EDIE, DAYTON	RA35795310	M/Sgt	Hqs Co, 179th Inf Regt

Headquarters Issuing Orders	Order Number: General	Order Number: Special	Date of Orders	Rescinded	Revoked	Amended	Corrected Copy
179th INF APO 86	30		31 July 1953				

Type of Award	Oak Leaf Clusters	O. L. C. Number
PURPLE HEART		

FOR WOUNDS RECEIVED IN ACTION IN in the vicinity of Mundung-ni, Korea on 11 July 1953 (Area) ON DATE OF

Remarks:

Entered the Federal service from California.

THE ADJUTANT GENERAL'S OFFICE. DECORATIONS AND AWARDS BRANCH. WASHINGTON. D. C.
RECORD OF AWARD OF PURPLE HEART

Purple Heart document, 31 July 1953.

```
GENERAL ORDERS                                    DEPARTMENT OF THE ARMY
NO. 30                             WASHINGTON 25, D. C., 26 April 1954
                              (EXTRACT)
       REPUBLIC OF KOREA PRESIDENTIAL UNIT CITATION.--The Republic of Korea
Presidential Unit Citation which was awarded by the Republic of Korea to
the following units of the United States Army is confirmed in accordance with
AR 220-315:

The 45th United States Infantry Division and attached units:
     45th Infantry Division
     179th Infantry

       REPUBLIC OF KOREA PRESIDENTIAL UNIT CITATION awarded by citation dated
30 September 1953, by Syngman Rhee, President of the Republic of Korea, for
exceptionally meritorious service to the Republic of Korea during the period
10 December 1951 to 31 July 1953, inclusive, with citation as follows:

       The 45th United States Infantry Division continually exhibited extra-
ordinary valor in combat and an unsurpassed excellence in the training and
coordinating of Republic of Korea forces.  In June 1952, the Division initiated
a series of brilliant surprise attacks in order to establish a formidable
outpost line beyond the existing main line of resistance and acquired many
new positions, including the now famous hill masses of "Eerie" and "Baldy."
The outposts were held securely in spite of the intense enemy counterattacks
to recapture the strategic sites.  Without yielding any of the newly acquired
gains, the Division inflicted heavy losses upon the foe before it was replaced
after over two hundred days of continuous combat.  At this point, the men of
the 45th United States Infantry Division undertook the important task of
technically training Republic of Korea troops.  Their efforts were rewarded
by a display of brilliant combat effectiveness throughout the Republic of
Korea forces.  The return to front line positions in September 1952 by the
Thunderbird Division created a new chapter in the military accomplishments
of both United States and Korean troops as the two fused and fought together
with a rare display of unity.  During the Communist summer offensive of 1953,
the 45th United States Infantry Division once again exhibited its fighting
spirit and singleness of purpose as it frustrated enemy attacks and preserved
vital positions on "Sand Bag Castle," "Heartbreak Ridge" and "Christmas Hill."
The steadfast devotion to duty, gallantry in battle and cooperative spirit
with which Republic of Korea troops were made an integral part of a unified
force reflect the greatest credit upon the 45th United States Infantry Division
and uphold the most esteemed traditions of the military profession.

       BY ORDER OF THE SECRETARY OF THE ARMY:

                                           M. B. RIDGWAY,
                                           General, United States Army
                                           Chief of Staff
OFFICIAL:
                                           A TRUE COPY:

JOHN A. KLEIN,
Major General, United States Army,
Acting The Adjutant General               R L MCGLASHAN
                                          WO JG     USA
```

Republic of Korea Presidential Unit Citation, 26 April 1954.

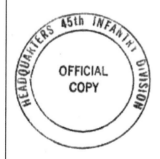

Bronze Star document.

Bronze Star document.

66th SIGNAL BN CORPS, FORT BRAGG, N.C. FEB 12, 1954 No 2

THE MEANING OF DISCIPLINE

"Discipline is what makes you do what you know you are supposed to do, or what is right from the point of view of the Army, despite any other inclination or desire you may have.

Discipline is something that works inside a person - we might call it an attitude, state of mind or 'a way of looking at things'. When we talk about the discipline of a unit, we mean simply the discipline of all members of that unit - the way everyone in the unit feels about the jobs the unit is given to do. If each man feels nothing is more important than the successful completion of his outfit's mission and is prepared to do whatever is necessary to see that it gets done, we have a disciplined unit. With this spirit, the unit functions as a team.

But if some members of an outfit don't see eye to eye with their fellow team members in this way, the whole team suffers and the sacrifices others have made could be wasted.

To win its battles and protect the efforts of conscientious soldiers, the Army insists that every member of a unit measure up to one high standard of discipline - to train and re-train until everyone looks at the team's job only one way - and that everyone performs as he should under all conditions.

This makes Army discipline a lot tougher for some men than it does for others. Some men come from homes or jobs that have required a high state of discipline from them. These men find the change from their previous standards to Army standards easy to make.

Others who have known little restraint in early life, find mea-
(cont)

M/SGT. AWARDED BRONZE STAR

At the weekly retreat parade on Friday, Feb. 5 M/Sgt. Dayton Edie of R & M Company was presented the Bronze Star Medal by Lt.Col. Willis E. Kooken, Battalion Commander.

M/Sgt. Edie received the award for his service with Headquarters Company, 179th Infantry Regiment, 45th Infantry Div. in Korea from Oct.10,1952 to July 27,1953.

An exerpt from the citation reads as follows:

"As communications chief, Sergeant Edie carried out his duties in a superior fashion. Often working under adverse conditions, he performed an unusually demanding complex of duties in an efficient and dependable manner. As a direct result of Sergeant Edie's initiative and technical skill, his unit maintained high morale and maximum combat effectiveness. His untiring efforts, resourcefulness, and sincere desire to serve enabled him to provide his unit with dependable service in any crisis. Sergeant Edie's competent efficiency and outstanding ability reflect great credit upon himself and the military service."

SAINTS NIP RAYS 84-75

Lee Field House last night was the scene of a hard fought battle in which the 66th Signal Rays came out on the short end against the Medics to the tune of 84-75.

The U.S.Army Hospital Saints who lead the battalion league came on with a second and third quarter rush to overcome an early Ray margin.

Paced by Smiley and Gregory, the Rays ran up a quick lead and at the quarter were in front by a 25-20 count. In the second stanza,
(cont)

Fort Bragg newsletter page, 12 February 1954.

Security Certificate, 27 May 1960.

RESTRICTED

HEADQUARTERS
TRIESTE UNITED STATES TROOPS
APO 209, US Army

SPECIAL ORDERS
NUMBER 133

9 June 1949

E X T R A C T

3. UP AR 615-5, fol EM, orgns indicated, are promoted to grades indicated.

TO BE MASTER SERGEANT

| Sgt lcl | Richard A Jeremias | RA12077188 | Cn Co 351 Inf (Dy 1st Sgt) |
| Sgt lcl | Charles V Smith | RA34472811 | 18th Sig Sv Co (Dy 1st Sgt) |

TO BE SERGEANT FIRST CLASS

Sgt Samuel W Gilliland   RA14024841   Hq Co 1st Bn 351st Inf

TO BE SERGEANT

Cpl	James A Campbell Jr	RA6863332	Hq Co 1st Bn 351st Inf
Cpl	Dayton Edie	RA35795310	18th Sig Sv Co
Cpl	Odean Evans	RA18124801	Company A 351st Inf
Cpl	James P Kyreakakis	RA32765624	Company B 351st Inf
Cpl	Gerald W Lowther	RA35396315	18th Sig Sv Co
Cpl	Billy C Sherwood	RA38733117	15th Tank Co
Cpl	Millard Snyder	RA12274989	Company B 351st Inf
Cpl	Darrell Thornley	RA38147547	Hq Co 2nd Bn 351st Inf
Cpl	Fredrick L Tobey	RA12116249	88th Mecz Cav Rcn Trp
Cpl	Ralph M Watson	RA18084746	18th Sig Sv Co
Cpl	Lewis H Wood	RA6936018	88th Mecz Cav Rcn Trp

BY COMMAND OF MAJOR GENERAL HOGE:

JOHN L WHITELAW
Col, GSC
CofS

OFFICIAL:

HARRY W ROBERTS
Captain AGD
Asst Adj Gen

DISTRIBUTION:
40 Misc Sec
3 Ea EM
15 351st Inf
3 15th Tank Co
3 88th Mecz Cav Rcn
5 18th Sig Sv Co

5 7178th Gen Dep
1 Ea Orders, Returns, ADC to CG, Os Sec
2 RTO
5 Fin O

RESTRICTED

Document shows Dayton's promotion to sergeant, 9 June 1949.

> CITATION
>
> The XVIII Airborne Corps Artillery Certificate of Achievement is awarded to Master Sergeant Dayton Edie, RA 35 795 310, Headquarters Battery, 54th Artillery Group, for meritorious Service as Communication Chief, Headquarters Battery, 54th Artillery Group, during the period 22 January 1964 to 30 April 1965. His proficiency and meticulous attention to detail in all aspects of his duties and his initiative in solving the many problems which confronted him were most commendable. His complete devotion to duty was shown by his willingness to work many long hours within the unit. Through his tact and courtesy, he established and maintained cordial relations with officers and noncommissioned officers of his unit and of higher headquarters. Master Sergeant Edie's personal leadership is reflected in his communication platoon greatly contributing to the superior rating achieved by Headquarters Battery, 54th Artillery Group in its last Annual General Inspection. During his tenure as Communications Chief, the communication platoon of his unit has been an efficient and combat ready platoon capable of accomplishing its mission in an outstanding manner. On the occasion of Sergeant Edie's retirement, after more than twenty years of faithful and honorable service, it is particularly noteworthy that he has participated in World War II and the Korean Conflict, in recognition of which he has been awarded numerous service and campaing medals. Master Sergeant Edie's outstanding performance of duty reflects great credit upon himself, his unit and the United States Army.

XVII Airborne Corps Artillery certificate, 22 January 1964.

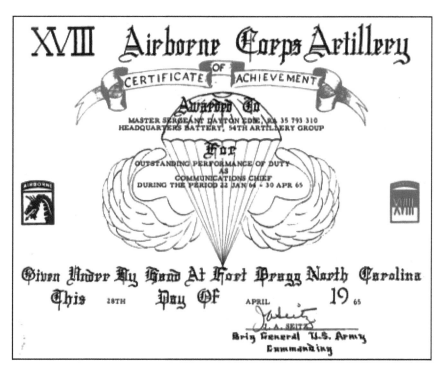

XVII Airborne Corps Artillery certificate, 22 January 1964.

FOR IMMEDIAT[illegible] [illegible]ELIVERY TO

Special Orders
No. 105

HEADQUARTERS,
DEPARTMENT OF THE ARMY,
Washington, D.C., *19 April 1965*

XXX XXX XXX

[illegible]4, TC [illegible]. DP fol indiv promoted and commissioned in AUS UP 10 US Code secs [illegible] and [illegible]. Commander will ntfy indiv.

GR (FR, TO) 1ST LT TO CAPT. DOR 19 Apr 1965.

SHAW, WILLIAM A., O[illegible] VO

XXX XXX XXX

[illegible], TC [illegible]. DP fol determinations pertaining to temp prm status indiv indic are [illegible]. Commander will ntfy indiv.

	Gr	DOR
RUSSELL, DEAN F., O[illegible] Arty	Capt	[illegible] May 1961

XXX XXX XXX

[illegible], TC [illegible]. Fol rsg dir. WP. TDN. PRAP AR [illegible] or AR [illegible] as approp and AR [illegible]. NATO tvl orders rqr by AR [illegible]. [illegible] P [illegible]. CIC [illegible]. Asg to USAOSREPLSTA ([illegible]) Ft Dix, NJ, for further asg USAREUR (Ger). Also Sep-471. Avail date 17 Sep 1965 to arr OS dest NLT [illegible] Sep 1965. Lv data [illegible] DDALVAHP. PCS (MDC) 4A. EDCSA 17 Sep 1965.

WASSEL, RAYMOND F., O[illegible] MAJ TC [illegible] ([illegible]) HHD [illegible] Trans Bn (Trk) Ft Bragg, NC, [illegible].

XXX XXX XXX

[illegible], TC [illegible]. UP 10 US Code [illegible] ([illegible]-yr retirement) indiv rel fr act dy on EDCSA. On date immed fol EDCSA indiv is placed on ret list trf to USAR (Retired Reserve) and asg to USAR Cont Gp (Ret) USAAC, St. Louis, Mo, [illegible]. SPN [illegible]. HOSTWOY. PCS. TDN. PPSIA. [illegible] P [illegible].

Name, current grade, SN and MOS	EDCSA	Date retired	Place of retirement
EDIE, DAYTON (NMN), MSGT (E-[illegible]) RA[illegible] MOS [illegible]	[illegible] Apr. 1965	1 May 1965	Ft Bragg, NC.

XXX XXX XXX

By Order of the Secretary of the Army:

HAROLD K. JOHNSON,
General, United States Army,
Chief of Staff.

Official:
J. C. LAMBERT,
Major General, United States Army,
The Adjutant General.

A TRUE EXTRACT COPY:

CHRISTOPHER S. CARLSON
2d Lt, AGC

RET RES

4-1070-F

Special Orders, HQ Washington, D.C., 19 April 1965.

Enlisted Record and Report of Separation document, 1 June 1946.

Re-enlistment document, 16 May 1952.

```
FOR IMMEDIATE DELIVERY TO:

              HEADQUARTERS US ARMY ARMOR CENTER
                     Fort Knox, Kentucky

SPECIAL ORDERS                                    24 November 1961
NUMBER    255        E X T R A C T
```

24. SMO DA Form 662 No 1259 this Hq 9 Nov 61 pert to TDY of LTCOL ERNEST L MEGGS 035474 Inf Hq USAARMS (2168) at Ft Benning Ga to attnd sp Inf Instr Conf to coord w/ C&S Dept USAIS the early dev of scopes and POI for the Career and associate Career crs which reads "2122020 52-1121 P2000-21/22 S15-014 (CDA 2110.1121)" IATR "2122020 53-1001 P2000-21 S09-038 2110.1119 (36-210) (limitation $97.00). 2122020 52-1121 P2000-21/22 S15-014 (CDA 2110.1121)" and the order is further amended to add "3 DDALV rtn journey." Req No 929.

25. DA Form 662 No 1256 this Hq 9 Nov 61 pert to TDY of LTCOL RICHARD J GLIKES 060197 Armor Hq USAARMS (2168) at Ft Benning Ga to coord w/ the C&S Dept USAIS the early dev of scopes and POI for the career and associate career crs is revo. Req No 931.

26. PVT-E1 OSCAR L MAYVILLE RA16685503 PMOS 31210 (CAU) Os Area & Tvl Sta Z ETS Nov 63 Profile A BPED Nov 60 RFA (PL) Co B 2d Bn Sch Regt USAARMS (2168) Ft Knox Ky (formerly stu 17-R-312.1 Cl No 8) and asg EUSA Pers Cen (5751) Korea APO 971 and WP USAOSREPLSTA (6020) OART Oakland Calif for trans. Prov AR 612-35 apply. Will rept OART Oakland Calif in unif prior to 1200 NLT 1 Dec 61. MWBAS Gr Name SN EUSA Pers Cen (5751) APO 971 San Francisco Calif. Auth Msg AGPA-DT 711169 TAG DA 10 Nov 61. TDN PCS-1P ACPATT 2122010 01-1261-1263 P1512 S99-999. CIC 221A03. TC will furn T and no meal tickets nec for journey. EDCSA 1 Dec 61 appl to unit of asg.

27. MSGT-E8 (P-1) DAYTON EDIE RA35795310 PMOS 31268 (CAU) Os Area & Tvl Sta B ETS Feb 63 Profile B Clnc TS Depn 2 AMOS 721 BPED Apr 43 RFA Co B 3d Bn Sch Regt USAARMS (2168) Ft Knox Ky and asg 2d BG 2d Inf APO 112 (0002) Gablingen Germany chg to USAREUR Sp-71 aloc and WP USAOSREPLSTA (1264) Ft Dix NJ for trans. Prov AR 612-35, para 7 AR 614-210, and para 3b and 6d AR 614-240 apply. 30 DDALVAHP. Will rept Ft Dix NJ prior to 1200 NLT 10 Jan 62. MWBAS Gr Name SN 2d BG 2d Inf (0002) APO 112 New York NY. Auth Ltr AGPA-M 201 Hq DA OTAG 14 Nov 61 Subj Asg Instr (Gr E8 E9) USAREUR Sp Rqn. TDN PCS-4A TPA PPSIA ACPATT 2122010 01-1461-1462-1463 P1514 S99-999. CIC 221A03. EDCSA 10 Jan 62 appl to unit of asg. NATO tvl order rqr.

28. FNE PMOS 42410 (CAU) FSAC L Os Area & Tvl Sta Z ETS Sep 62 Profile A RFA Co B 2d Bn Sch Regt USAARMS (2168) and asg 3d MTB 123d Armor. COA-99. EDCSA 6 Dec 61. Rec will be hand carried.

		BPED
PFC-E3 GORDON CHRISTMAS	NG23177374	Jul 60
SP4-E4 BILLY K LEE	NG23197207	Jan 60
SP4-E4 FULTON WATKINS JR	NG23189530	Oct 57

Extract Special Orders, 24 November 1961.

Security Certificate, 2 September 1963.

Security Certificate, 13 December 1963.

Service Data document, 17 May 1955.

Security Certificate, 29 January 1964.

```
                        HEADQUARTERS
                     54TH ARTILLERY GROUP
                   Fort Bragg, North Carolina 28307

SPECIAL ORDERS                                            18 March 1964
NUMBER    42

     1. TC 253. Fol DUTY ASSIGNMENT/RELIEF ann this sta. NTI.

JONES, GAINES E  W2211860  CWO W-2  USA  Svc Btry 3rd How Bn 16th Arty
  Dy asg:    NA
  Dy rel fr: Alternate custodian of Crypto Material
  Eff date:  4 Mar 64
  Sp instr:  NA

EDIE, DAYTON  RA35795310  MSG E-8  PA  Hq Btry 54th Arty Gp this sta
  Dy asg:    ADD DY-Alternate Custodian of Crypto Material
  Dy rel fr: NA
  Eff date:  4 Mar 64
  Sp instr:  Crypto Acct NR 937. DA Form 873 fwd TAG 27 Mat 60 NAC Compl
             by HQ US ARMY ARMOR CENTER, FORT KNOX, KY 1 Mar 49 Degree
             S cty Clnc "TOP SECRET.

     2. TC 255. Fol SPECIAL DUTY ASSIGNMENT ann this sta. NTI.

LILLY, AUBREY W  US54344520  PVT E-2  Hq Btry 54th Arty Gp this sta
  SD to:     Organizational Auto PM School
  Rept date: 23 Mar 64
  Period:    3 wks
  Purpose:   To attend Auto PM Crse #143-E
  Sp instr:  EM will rept to Post Auto Maint Sch at 0730 hrs 23 Mar 64

          FOR THE COMMANDER:

                                          [signature]

                                          CHARLES D. SMITH
                                          Major, Artillery
                                          Adjutant

DISTRIBUTION:
  "S"
```

Special Orders, HQ, Fort Bragg, 18 March 1964.

```
                          HEADQUARTERS
                        54TH ARTILLERY GROUP
                      Fort Bragg, North Carolina 28307

SPECIAL ORDERS                                          11 September 1964
NUMBER      128

     1.  TC 322.  UP AR 672-5-1 fol indiv this sta qual and badge--crse--
weapon--score indic awd BADGES INDIC.  EM qualified 9 Sep 64.
             EXPERT BADGE w/
ALLEN, HUGH C  05314960  1ST LT  MSC  Hq Btry 54th Arty Gp
         Weapon:  Cal 45 Pistol  Score:  358  CRS:  I
SNYDER, FRANCIS N  US51496648  SP4 E-4  Hq Btry 54th Arty Gp
         Weapon:  Cal 45 Pistol  Score:  359  CRS:  I

     2.  TC 255.  Fol SPECIAL DUTY ASSIGNMENT ann this sta.

EDIE, DAYTON  R135795310  MSG E-8  Hq Btry 54th Arty Gp
  SD to:  Commo Security Equip Op School
  Rept date:  14 Sep 64
  Pd:  5 days
  Scty clnc:  TS
  Sp instr:  Rpt to Bldg 20-S-4040, RTC Area between the hours of 1300-1600
             on 11 Sep 64.

     3.  TC 327.  Fol MOS action dir.

WALSH, PATRICK W  RA16595692  SP4 E-4  Hq Btry 54th Arty Gp
  Awd:  P671.10
  Wd:   P670.00
  Auth: AR 611-203

CRANDELL, STEPHEN G  RA19726387  SP4 E-4  Hq Btry 54th Arty Gp
  Awd:  P310.00  S635.10
  Wd:   P635.10
  Auth: AR 611-203

     4.  TC 253.  Fol DUTY ASSIGNMENT/RELIEF ann this sta.  NTI.

ZAHRLY, JACK H  05317610  2D LT  ARTY  HQ 54th Arty Gp
  Dy asg:  PDY-Commo Off  (MOS 0200)
  Dy rel Fr:  PDY-Casual  (MOS 0001)
  Eff date:  11 Sep 64

             FOR THE COMMANDER:

                                        Charles D. Smith
                                        CHARLES D. SMITH
                                        Major, Artillery
                                        Adjutant

DISTRIBUTION:
    "S"
```

Special Orders, HQ, Fort Bragg, 11 September 1964.

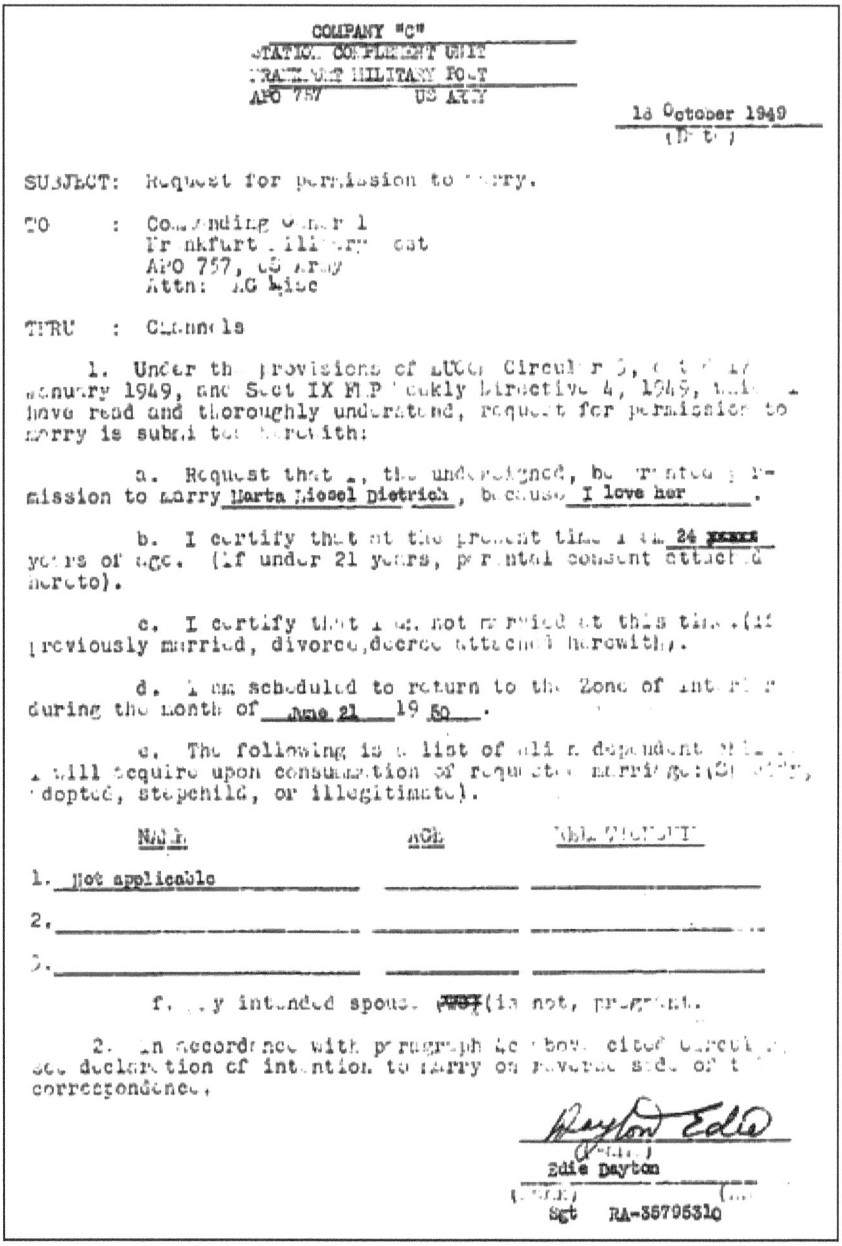

COMPANY "C"
STATION COMPLEMENT UNIT
FRANKFURT MILITARY POST
APO 757 US ARMY

18 October 1949
(Date)

SUBJECT: Request for permission to marry.

TO : Commanding General
Frankfurt Military Post
APO 757, US Army
Attn: AG Misc

THRU : Channels

1. Under the provisions of EUCOM Circular 5, dated 17 January 1949, and Sect IX FMP Weekly Directive 4, 1949, which I have read and thoroughly understand, request for permission to marry is submitted herewith:

a. Request that I, the undersigned, be granted permission to marry Marta Liesel Dietrich, because I love her.

b. I certify that at the present time I am 24 years of age. (If under 21 years, parental consent attached hereto).

c. I certify that I am not married at this time. (If previously married, divorce decree attached herewith).

d. I am scheduled to return to the Zone of Interior during the month of June 21 1950.

e. The following is a list of alien dependents which I will acquire upon consummation of requested marriage: (Children, adopted, stepchild, or illegitimate).

NAME	AGE	RELATIONSHIP
1. Not applicable		
2.		
3.		

f. My intended spouse (is not) pregnant.

2. In accordance with paragraph 4c above cited directive, see declaration of intention to marry on reverse side of this correspondence.

Dayton Edie
(Signature)
Edie Dayton
(Name)
Sgt RA-35795310

Because 'I Love Her' document, 18 October 1949.

18 October 1949

SUBJECT: Letter of Acquiescence

TO : Commanding General
Frankfurt Military Post
APO 757, US Army
Attn: AG Misc

THRU : Channels

1. Under the provisions of EUCOM Circular 3, dated 17 January 1949, and Sect IX, F.M. Weekly Directive 4, 1949, which I have read and thoroughly understand, the following is submitted:

   a. I, THE UNDERSIGNED,

   NAME _Miss Marta Liesel Dietrich_

   RANK _not applic_ ASN or ACO _not applic_

   Age _23_ Nationality _German_

   Present Marital Status _Single_

   Place of Employment _Schoolteacher, Nordenstadt, b Wiesbaden_

   Address _31 Altstadtstrasse Diez/Lahn, Germany_

   b. WISH TO MARRY,

   NAME _Edio Dayton_
   RANK _Sergeant_ ASN or Serial No. _RA-35790510_
   Age _24_ Nationality _American_
   Present Marital Status _Single_
   Place of Employment _US Army_
   Address _Co G 7811 SCU, MP, APO 757_
   c/o P: N.Y. New York

   c. BECAUSE, _I love him_

   d. I understand that marriage to a citizen of the United States does not confer United States Citizenship upon an alien under existing laws, although it does facilitate the alien's entry into the United States and naturalization after taking up residence there.

   e. I understand that I will be entitled to such allowances, allotment insurance and other benefits as are authorized by law upon completion of marriage.

   f. I understand that I will not be entitled to any privileges including commissary, Post Exchange, Government quarters, medical or dental services not accorded prior to marriage, except as may be authorized by EUCOM directives.

   g. I understand that military personnel are subject to transfer and change of station in accordance with the exigencies of the service.

Because 'I Love Him' document, 18 October 1949.

Meritorious Achievement or Service document, 15 August 1953.

Meritorious Achievement or Service document, 15 August 1953.

Service Record, 17 May 1946 - May 1949.

SECTION 9—REMARKS—ADMINISTRATIVE

DATE	REMARK	DATE	REMARK
17 May 46	Enl Auth WD Cir 110-46		
	— Not Used —		
	Amendment of National Service Life Ins. Act explained to soldier		
	— Not Used —		
	Primary MOS determined as 667 by Class Bd. Cir 211, WD, 47, acceptable. /s/ Clayton Edie		
30 Nov 48	AC Completed 19 Oct 48 - Report filed Hq TRUST APO 209		
4 Apr 49	PBI (Cryptographic) Completed 1 Mar 49 Report Filed G-2, HQ TRUST APO 209 U S Army		
16 May 49	36 mos continuous sv toward GCM.		
16 May 49	Character - Excellent Efficiency rating - Superior		

Service Record, 17 May 1946 - May 1949.

Old marker for Dayton Edie.

Arlington National Cemetery
Arlington, Arlington County, Virginia, USA
Section 55, Site 3896

Photo by Paul Hays

New marker for Dayton Edie.